DEVIL'S ADVOCA

M000164676

DEVIL'S ADVOCATES is a series of books devoted to exploring the classics of horror cinema. Contributors to the series come from the fields of teaching, academia, journalism and fiction, but all have one thing in common: a passion for the horror film and a desire to share it with the widest possible audience.

'The admirable Devil's Advocates series is not only essential – and fun – reading for the serious horror fan but should be set texts on any genre course.'
Dr Ian Hunter, Professor of Film Studies, De Montfort University, Leicester

'Auteur Publishing's new Devil's Advocates critiques on individual titles... offer bracingly fresh perspectives from passionate writers. The series will perfectly complement the BFI archive volumes.' **Christopher Fowler,** *Independent on Sunday*

'Devil's Advocates has proven itself more than capable of producing impassioned, intelligent analyses of genre cinema... quickly becoming the go-to guys for intelligent, easily digestible film criticism.' *Horror Talk.com*

'Auteur Publishing continue the good work of giving serious critical attention to significant horror films.' *Black Static*

 DevilsAdvocatesbooks

DevilsAdBooks

ALSO AVAILABLE IN THIS SERIES

Antichrist Amy Simmonds

Black Sunday Martyn Conterio

The Blair Witch Project Peter Turner

Candyman Jon Towlson

Cannibal Holocaust Calum Waddell

Carrie Neil Mitchell

The Company of Wolves James Gracey

The Curse of Frankenstein Marcus K. Harmes

Dead of Night Jez Conolly & David Bates

The Descent James Marriot

Don't Look Now Jessica Gildersleeve

Frenzy Ian Cooper

Halloween Murray Leeder

Ju-on The Grudge Marisa Hayes

Let the Right One In Anne Billson

Macbeth Rebekah Owens

Nosferatu Cristina Massaccesi

Saw Benjamin Poole

The Shining Laura Mee

The Silence of the Lambs Barry Forshaw

Suspiria Alexandra Heller-Nicholas

The Texas Chain Saw Massacre James Rose

The Thing Jez Conolly

Witchfinder General Ian Cooper

FORTHCOMING

Daughters of Darkness Kat Ellinger

The Devils Darren Arnold

House of Usher Evert van Leeuwen

The Fly Emma Westwood

It Follows Joshua Grimm

Psychomania I.Q. Hunter & Jamie Sherry

Scream Steven West

Twin Peaks: Fire Walk With Me Lindsay Hallam

DEVIL'S ADVOCATES

IN THE MOUTH OF MADNESS

MICHAEL BLYTH

Acknowledgments

Firstly, I would like to thank John Atkinson at Auteur for his generous support and undying patience – and for saying yes to this thing in the first place. I would also like to express my gratitude to Duncan Carson and Daniel Cockburn, for sharing both their precious time and their infinite wisdom with me.

But mostly, I would like to thank David Edgar, who never, ever imagined he would spend so much time talking about this film. I couldn't have done it without you, David – thank you for being the smartest person I know.

First published in 2018 by
Auteur, 24 Hartwell Crescent, Leighton Buzzard LU7 1NP
www.auteur.co.uk
Copyright © Auteur 2018

Series design: Nikki Hamlett at Cassels Design
Set by Cassels Design www.casselsdesign.co.uk
Printed and bound in Great Britain

British Library Cataloguing-in-Publication Data
A catalogue record for this book is available from the British Library

ISBN paperback: 978-1-911325-40-6
ISBN ebook: 978-1-911325-41-3

CONTENTS

Introduction: 'Maybe He's Too Sophisticated For You?'...7

Chapter 1: 'It's Just a Matter of Time'...13

Chapter 2: 'Do You Like My Ending?'...19

Chapter 3: 'All Those Horrible, Slimy Things'...35

Chapter 4: 'You Can Forget About Stephen King'..53

Chapter 5: 'The New Bible'...67

Chapter 6: 'Isn't He the Guy Who Writes that Horror Crap?'...77

Chapter 7: 'This One Will Drive You Absolutely Mad'...91

Conclusion: 'This is a Rotten Way to End It'..105

Bibliography...107

INTRODUCTION: 'MAYBE HE'S TOO SOPHISTICATED FOR YOU?'

John Carpenter has always been a little ahead of his time. It seems an odd thing to say about a filmmaker whose work so often looks to the past for inspiration, be that in his frequent homages to old-school Hollywood Westerns, or affectionate nods to the tinfoil kitsch of vintage science fiction B-movies. But it is not so much the films themselves that boast prophetic qualities, rather the fact that it seems to take everyone else a bit of time to catch up with his vision. Of course, I am referring to the often genre-phobic critical establishment who time and time again tore into Carpenter's films upon their initial release, only to turn around years later and herald them as bona fide celluloid classics. A case in point is Vincent Canby's scathing review of *The Thing* (1982), originally published in the New York Times. Canby vented:

> *The Thing* is a foolish, depressing, overproduced movie that mixes horror with science fiction to make something that is fun as neither one thing or the other. Sometimes it looks as if it aspired to be the quintessential moron movie of the 80's. (Canby, 1982)

It is hard to fathom that Canby's opinion was representative of an overwhelmingly negative critical consensus toward *The Thing* at the time, but then critics do have a habit of backtracking – particularly when it comes to recognising the cultural value of popular horror cinema. Today the film is regarded a classic – and not just a cult classic, but a genre institution that demonstrates the artistic and intellectual capacities of sci-fi and horror. Not only is it a regular fixture in lists of the 'greatest sci-fi movies' or 'most terrifying pictures ever made', but also the continued topic of academic and literary study. Rather impressive for a 'quintessential moron movie'.

Now widely regarded as the defining text in the slasher sub-genre, even Carpenter's game-changing *Halloween* (1978) was met with suspicion amongst horror-shy critics when it first emerged. For every review that gave praise to Carpenter's technical skill and handling of suspense, another would label it an innocuous slice of horror trash, worthy only of derision. Pauline Kael at the New Yorker fell regrettably into the latter camp, lamenting the film's *'pitiful, amateurish script'* (Kael, 1979), before ultimately labelling

7

it a mindless exercise in repetition, '*stripped of everything but dumb scariness*' (ibid.).

Meanwhile, fan-favourite *Prince of Darkness* (1987), a film about which critical opinion has changed markedly over the years (and continues to do so with increasing rapidity), was met with similar hostility when it debuted almost a decade after the release of *Halloween*. In a particularly snooty Washington Post review, Richard Harrington said simply '*The* [sic] Prince of Darkness *stinks*' (Harrington, 1987), and, poking fun at the evil green goo at the film's centre, argued that '*it too deserves to be shut up in a canister for 7 million years*' (ibid.).

The list of bad reviews for Carpenter films now deemed as classics could go on (and on), but it was by no means just the critics who gave him a needlessly hard time; audiences too seemed reticent to embrace his creations. Rather surprisingly, many of his most beloved films – *Assault on Precinct 13* (1976), *The Fog* (1980), *Christine* (1983) and *Big Trouble in Little China* (1986) among them – failed to attract cinema-goers, initially proving to be financial flops, which took a toll on Carpenter's perceived commercial credibility.

Still, there is no use in dwelling on the past, and while much of Carpenter's work may not have opened to rave reviews or round the block queues, time has largely redressed the balance and ensured that many of his once overlooked masterworks are now rightfully regarded as such. But while Carpenter's films have a history of taking time to warm up, there is one particular outing that is yet to receive the full recognition it deserves: *In the Mouth of Madness*.

When the film opened in 1995 it received a response sadly all too familiar for Carpenter: one of general indifference. In a largely lacklustre review, Roger Ebert said '*One wonders how* In the Mouth of Madness *might have turned out if the script had contained even a little more wit and ambition*' (Ebert, 1995). Flagrantly disregarding the film's conceptual scope and narrative complexities, Ebert's review was representative of a frustratingly predictable critical refusal to engage with the film on an intellectual level – much like Pauline Kael, he seemed closed off to the idea that a horror movie could offer something smart, something other than 'dumb' scares. While *In the Mouth of Madness* has collected its fair share of admirers along the way, it has not received anywhere near the critical and academic reassessment afforded to other Carpenter

classics, and therein lies the reason for this book – to reappraise and reclaim a film still undervalued by horror fans and critics alike, and rightly position it as one of John Carpenter's most accomplished and compelling pieces of work.

In their book on the director, Colin Odell and Michelle LeBlanc offered a hopeful thought, arguing that, *'Of all the genres, horror is the swiftest in reacting to new trends, as well as plundering its rich heritage, so there's a possibility that* In the Mouth of Madness' *complexity may well be re-evaluated'* (Le Blanc and Odell, 2011: 25).

Well, let's give it a try.

I intend to begin proceedings by giving some context as to the cinematic horror landscape at the time *In the Mouth of Madness* was first released (arguably one of the biggest lulls that the genre has ever seen), possibly explaining why the film was so unfairly neglected in 1995. As the passing of time continues to uncover the many nuances of Carpenter's film, not to mention establish it as a formative text in the evolution of the postmodernism boom in contemporary horror cinema at the turn of the century, it could be argued that the film was the unfortunate victim of an era that just did not care for horror, and its lack of initial success simply a matter of bad timing.

Next, I will place the film specifically within the context of Carpenter's wider filmography, exploring not only how it incorporates and builds on many of the ideas that he has explored throughout his career, but also the ways in which it differs and stands apart from his other works. *In the Mouth of Madness* marks the climax of the director's self-named 'Apocalypse Trilogy', preceded by *The Thing* and *Prince of Darkness*, whilst it also speaks to his wider eschatological preoccupations, as well recurring Carpenterian themes around the loss of free will, a paranoid distrust of mass industry and global corporations, and the cataclysmic resurgence of an ancient evil. But while the themes of the film are classic Carpenter, artistically it represents a departure from some of his most recognisable stylistic trademarks, namely his editing, camerawork and use of music.

From there I will go on to discuss how *In the Mouth of Madness* serves as a direct tribute to the writings of H.P. Lovecraft, examining how his influence shapes the narrative structure and conceptual ideologies of the film. Comparing it to other cinematic adaptations of Lovecraft's work, I will argue that Carpenter's film displays a rare understanding of Lovecraftian ideologies, offering up a rich cinematic conceptualisation of his distinct brand of cosmic horror, despite not being based on any one specific Lovecraft text. Throughout this chapter I intend to not only examine the different ways Carpenter makes explicit reference to numerous Lovecraft works, but suggest why the scribe's writing style has proved so problematic for filmmakers to translate to the screen, and how Carpenter tackles this problem in a number of imaginative and intelligent ways.

More than just a tribute to Lovecraft, *In the Mouth of Madness* is also heavily indebted to the work of Stephen King, and in Chapter 4 I will look at the ways King's fiction, and his own celebrity persona, informs Carpenter's film. I will position the film within the broader context of the gothic literary tradition, before exploring the ways in which it subverts the traditional idea of the literary adaptation, not just in terms of narrative, but also in the many visual tricks it employs to represent the written word on screen.

Then I will explore religion as a common motif employed throughout the film. As with many Western horror films, Christianity serves as a theological foundation, but Carpenter's film also draws interesting parallels with the Church of Scientology. I intend to explore the ways in which the character of novelist Sutter Cane represents an L. Ron Hubbard-like figure; a writer of science-fiction whose work has taken on religious significance among devoted followers.

Next, I will discuss the various modes of self-reflexivity evident in the film, and how they are used to create meaning and subvert audience expectations. *In the Mouth of Madness* is not only a tribute to Lovecraft and an *homage* to King, it is also a film in which Carpenter references and critiques his own body of work and his position as purveyor of the horrific and macabre. By blurring the lines between fantasy and reality, and in turn, the lines between sanity and madness, *In the Mouth of Madness* becomes a film about the very nature of horror and highlights the ways in which the genre is perhaps the most consistently reflexive of all cinematic forms.

Lastly, I plan to explore the film's ontological concerns by focusing on its radical (and unnerving) aesthetic and philosophical disorientations: the non-linear presentation of time, cyclical narratives and visual repetition, and the fundamental distrust of perception (seeing as believing and seeing as deception).

CHAPTER 1: 'IT'S JUST A MATTER OF TIME'

When considering the critical and commercial responses to *In the Mouth of Madness* when it was released in 1995, it is important first and foremost to look at the cinematic climate of the time, and ask if the state of the horror genre was in some ways indicative of (and responsible for) the lacklustre response with which it was initially met.

It is often acknowledged among horror fans that the early 1990s was not the strongest period in the genre's history. In fact, it has been argued that the first half of the decade represented one of the most significant lulls that US horror cinema has been witness to, with the volume of film production, box office takings and overall audience interest hitting an all-time low. Of course, such lulls can only ever really come after a boom, and the previous decade had been a highly prolific and profitable time for the genre. But while the 1980s were littered with innovative horror classics, it is also recognised as the era of the sequel, a time when the franchise reigned supreme and horror cinema became less about striving for new ideas than the increasingly cynical (but lucrative) expansion of those which had come before. Michael, Jason and Freddy, would you please stand up.

If the 1980s was the decade of the sequel, it was the slasher craze that served as the primary catalyst. While stalk and slash precursors such as Bob Clark's *Black Christmas* (1974) or Mario Bava's perverse eco-shocker *A Twitch of the Death Nerve* (1971) (aka *A Bay of Blood*) paved the way, it was Carpenter's *Halloween* that perfected the model. Setting his mayhem within an exclusively teenage milieu, Carpenter struck box office gold, and, crucially, set the rules (if only inadvertently) that would define the highly-profitable horror sub-genre for years to come. Hot on Carpenter's heels, and with its eye firmly on the same box office gold, Sean Cunningham's *Friday the 13th* (1980) emerged, streamlining Carpenter's original formula (ditching character development and upping the gore quote along the way) to create a box office behemoth. And of course, Wes Craven threw his own homicidal pop-culture icon into the mix, in the form of hypnagogic child killer Freddy Krueger, when his imaginative riff on the slasher formula *A Nightmare on Elm Street* (1984) captured the imaginations of bloodthirsty filmgoers.

What would follow over the course of the 1980s was, to many, a sustained exercise in diminishing returns. In an attempt to cash in on the popularity of their originators, sequels for the three predominant franchises were churned out at regular intervals, leaving many cinema-goers disillusioned by the directions in which they were headed. Carpenter himself worked on both the first two *Halloween* sequels, before completely removing himself from the ongoing franchise. With this in mind, one might consider the reflexive (even critical) *In the Mouth of Madness* his rumination on the business of horror and the cynical commercialisation of the horror franchise. But more on that later…

Countless other body count movies emerged during this time, ranging from the good – *Happy Birthday To Me* (1981), *The Burning* (1981), *Slumber Party Massacre* (1982), *Sleepaway Camp* (1983), to the bad – *Don't Go in the Woods* (1981), *Pieces* (1982), *Nail Gun Massacre* (1985), to the downright bizarre – *Crazy Fat Ethel 2* (1987) anyone? – but by the end of the decade the boom had been reduced to merely a whimper, and in its desperate attempts to keep fresh blood flowing, the sub-genre had drifted dangerously far from the simplicity and elegance of Carpenter's iconoclastic trend-setter.

So here we were at the beginning of a new decade: the 1990s. Both *Halloween* and *A Nightmare on Elm Street* had hit number five in their respective series, while *Friday the 13th* had accumulated an unprecedented eight entries, what with Jason having just recently (albeit tepidly) taken Manhattan. And while such well-established franchises limped slowly toward their graves, the output of some of the genre's former directorial superstars was not looking much sprightlier. The 1970s had witnessed the emergence of a new generation of horror filmmakers who established themselves outside of the main studio system. But while early commercial success and critical acclaim came quickly for Carpenter's peers, few of these figures could parlay their initial success into subsequent creative or commercial hits. Tobe Hooper, for example, the man behind *The Texas Chain Saw Massacre* (1974), found unexpected mainstream success in the early 1980s with the Steven Spielberg-produced family shocker *Poltergeist* (1982), but struggled in the latter half of the decade, with films such as *Lifeforce* (1985) and *Invaders From Mars* (1986) proving critical and financial flops (although both have gone on to achieve a degree of cult status, particularly the sci-fi sauciness of the former). But those disappointments were nothing compared to the horrors of the 1990s, during which Hooper made a series of missteps, including *Spontaneous Combustion* (1990), *Night Terrors* (1993) and *The Mangler* (1995). George A. Romero was also facing problems of his own. Having run into difficulties working for a major studio, the devoutly independent Romero embarked on a seven-year hiatus following bad experiences on both *Monkey Shines* (1988) and *The Dark Half* (1993). Perhaps for the likes of Hooper and Romero, who had produced their most iconic works independently, subsequent collaborations with big studios proved an awkward fit, resulting in a somewhat compromised or even diluted version of what had come before? And as if this wasn't bad enough, beloved purveyor of the perverse David Cronenberg had all but ditched the horror genre with the advent of the new decade in favour of his idiosyncratic new brand of psychological dramas. And let us not forget William Friedkin's much-touted return to horror, *The Guardian* (1990), a preposterous nanny-from-hell shocker which offered little to rival the glowing reputation of his acclaimed *The Exorcist* (1973).

Faced with the whimpering tail end of a commercial boom and relentless critical dismissal, horror cinema attempted a makeover of sorts, pointedly targeting the thirtysomething young professional market, as opposed to the gore-hungry teen crowd. Following in Cronenberg's footsteps, the genre moved towards the classier terrains of the 'psychological thriller' (albeit in more palatable ways than the outré Canadian auteur), and yuppie peril films like *The Hand That Rocks the Cradle* (1992), *Pacific Heights* (1990) and *Single White Female* (1992) made a killing at the box office. Elsewhere the scuzzy disreputability of the slasher genre gave way to a return of the gothic, with a stream of big budget studio adaptations of literary horror classics such as *Bram Stoker's Dracula* (1992) and *Mary Shelley's Frankenstein* (1994). Meanwhile the likes of *Misery* (1990), *The Silence of the Lambs* (1991) and *Wolf* (1994) all boasted high production values and A-list stars, nudging the genre towards mainstream acceptability and awards season friendliness.

That is not to say that there was a complete drought of interesting and unapologetic genre films during the early part of the decade. Wes Craven proved that not all of horror's heavyweights were down and out when he injected the Freddy franchise with a much-needed dose of intelligence and originality in the form of *Wes Craven's New Nightmare* (1994) (a film we will return to later on in this book). Other notable works from the period included Bernard Rose's adaptation of a Clive Barker short story,

Candyman (1992), Barker's own sophomore directorial endeavour *Nightbreed* (1990),
Richard Stanley's ingenious slice of techno terror *Hardware* (1990) and William Peter
Blatty's *The Exorcist III* (1990), an unexpectedly effective entry in the series, especially
considering the widely accepted disaster that was the second instalment. However, while
these films were met with a degree of critical acclaim, with the exception of *Candyman*,
they did not prove commercially successful, hitting the radars of only the most dedicated
genre connoisseurs.

John Carpenter himself recognised the genre's descent into mediocrity. Speaking to
Fangoria in the run-up to the release of *In the Mouth of Madness*, he said:

> It's a really bad time for horror… A lot of techniques have been stolen by mainstream
> action pictures… What horror has to do, as far as I'm concerned, is turn a new
> corner and come up with something fresh. So I think we're all waiting for a redefining
> of the horror film… We need a *2001*. We need to do for horror what *2001* did for
> science fiction. (Carpenter in Rowe, 1995)

For many, that new corner was turned in the latter half of the decade when meta-
slasher *Scream* (1996) and, a few years later, found-footage faux documentary *The Blair
Witch Project* (1999) hit big, refreshing the flagging genre and once again proving horror
cinema as a legitimate commercial viability. Expanding on the self-reflexivity of *New
Nightmare*, Wes Craven's *Scream* featured a line-up of genre-savvy teens who had grown
up watching the director's own Freddy flicks, as well as Carpenter's iconic *Halloween* and
the countless slashers like *Prom Night* (1980) and *Terror Train* (1980) which followed in
its wake. No longer did audiences need to roll their eyes at the well-worn genre clichés
on display, because the characters on screen were doing the eye-rolling for us. While
Scream drew from familiar horror narratives, *The Blair Witch Project* had its sights set on
formal innovation, with its vérité approach giving birth to the found-footage trend. In
reality, neither *Scream* nor *The Blair Witch Project* were doing anything particularly new.
Cine-literate victims had already scoffed their way through the likes of unsophisticated
early slasher parodies *Student Bodies* (1981) or *Return to Horror High* (1987), or even
the aforementioned *New Nightmare*, in which Craven's characters existed in a world
where the *Elm Street* franchise was an everyday part of popular consciousness. Likewise,
the debt of *The Blair Witch Project* can be traced as far back as Ruggero Deodato's

anthropological exploitationer *Cannibal Holocaust* (1980), or as recently as pseudo-documentary *The Last Broadcast* (1998), in which a film crew run into trouble in their search for the Jersey Devil. While neither *Scream* nor *The Blair Witch Project* were exactly ground-breaking, they hit at just the right time to take the world by storm and double-handedly revive the genre from near extinction.

In many ways *In the Mouth of Madness* anticipated the winking self-reflexivity of *Scream*, creating a world in which its characters are aware of the tropes and conventions of the horror genre. But while *Scream* achieved this by having its characters make direct reference to films that had come before, *In the Mouth of Madness* was a more sophisticated think-piece on horror, exploring the deep philosophical and socio-political implications of a then unfashionable genre. It is not hard to see why the relative simplicity of *Scream* proved such an appealing prospect for audiences: it replicated the fun of the slasher with an added knowingness that was hip and easy to understand, presenting a playful and ultimately uncomplicated brand of postmodernism. *In the Mouth of Madness* did not have hot teens or a (soon to be iconic) masked killer, but instead featured middle-aged protagonists and a plot centring on literary intrigue. And, crucially, it was trying to lure audiences down a much deeper rabbit hole, philosophically speaking. *In the Mouth of Madness* was just not sexy enough, and its observations about horror too cerebral for it to be the corner-turning movie to end the horror drought of the early 90s. It may well have been met with more open arms had it emerged in a post-*Scream* world when horror could be cool, relevant and, most importantly, clever. Perhaps in a more enlightened landscape, audiences and critics might have taken a bit more time to unpack the complicated pleasures of Carpenter's film?

Furthermore, not only did *In the Mouth of Madness* debut during the closing moments of this significant horror depression, it came at a time when no one was expecting great things from its director. This was Carpenter's first feature film since the disappointing *Memoirs of an Invisible Man* (1992), which had been widely panned (even by Carpenter standards) upon its release. The following year he worked with Tobe Hooper on the enjoyable, if slight, TV anthology horror *Body Bags* (1993), which caused barely a ripple. It would be fair to say that by the time *In the Mouth of Madness* arrived the wider mainstream was not exactly waiting with baited breath for the next John Carpenter joint.

But while *In the Mouth of Madness* debuted at an inauspicious time for horror, a time which almost dictated it would fail, interestingly, the film is in and of itself a call to arms for the beleaguered genre. This tale of a missing horror novelist, whose writing is reported to have severe side effects for its readers, was a veritable love letter to Carpenter's cherished genre, and his own personal plea to be taken seriously as a filmmaker. The film was a meditation on the importance of horror as one of the world's most nimble forms of storytelling, and a warning on what could result should the genre not be given the respect it deserves. Sadly, while the timing was somewhat perfect, no-one was listening.

As such, *In the Mouth of Madness* is about as close as Carpenter might get to a lost film. It is the one that got away, the film that deserves to be mentioned in the same breath as *Halloween* or *The Fog* or *Escape from New York* (1981), but for one reason or another, rarely is. Numerous books have been written on Carpenter's career, countless chapters in a multitude of academic journals explore his filmmaking style and offer theoretical readings of his work, and of course there are the texts which focus purely on individual Carpenter films (two of which have already emerged as part of this Devil's Advocates series in the form of Jez Conolly's exemplary study of *The Thing* and Murray Leeder's exhaustive reading of *Halloween*). Yet in amongst this treasure trove of commentaries devoted to Carpenter's oeuvre, surprisingly few dwell on *In the Mouth of Madness*, which seems to merit little more than the occasional footnote. That may well have been down to timing, but, if anything, the years have been kind to this particular film, which feels more prescient, more essential and more daringly complex than ever. The time has finally come to take a long, hard look inside this mouth of madness. Open wide…

CHAPTER 2: 'DO YOU LIKE MY ENDING?'

Given that John Carpenter's *In the Mouth of Madness* can be a somewhat elusive beast, narratively speaking – rife with inset narratives and disorienting false turns – a plot summary might be useful before we begin to unpack the film's many pleasures and complexities. So, for those of you in need of a quick recap, here we go…

SYNOPSIS

We begin with a man named John Trent (Sam Neill) being dragged, kicking and screaming, into a high security psychiatric institution. Thrown inside a padded cell, Trent is visited by Dr Wrenn (David Warner), to whom he recounts the strange events that led to his incarceration.

In an extended flashback, we learn that Trent is an insurance fraud investigator. After surviving a seemingly random attack by an axe-wielding maniac, Trent is hired by Arcane Publishing to locate missing horror novelist Sutter Cane (Jürgen Prochnow). At a meeting with company director Jackson Harglow (Charlton Heston), Trent is told how Cane's hugely successful work has been known to have psychotic effects on unstable readers, and that his recent attacker was Cane's former agent. Harglow assigns Cane's editor, Linda Styles (Julie Carmen), to accompany Trent in his search for the absent writer.

As Trent immerses himself in Cane's literature for research purposes, he begins to experience nightmares which bleed into his waking life. Meanwhile, he notices a pattern on the artwork of Cane's books, which form a map of Hobb's End, the fictional location of Cane's stories. Concerned Cane's disappearance is all part of a publicity stunt, Trent, along with Styles, sets out to find Hobb's End. As they drive through the night the pair encounter a series of bizarre visions, before inexplicably arriving in the supposedly fictional town, which appears exactly as Cane describes it in his novels.

Trent and Styles check in to a local inn, run by a sweet old lady who claims to have never heard of Cane. The pair visit a huge Byzantine church, like the one described in Cane's novel *The Hobb's End Horror*, where they encounter a gang of angry townsfolk, demanding to see Cane. Suddenly the doors of the church burst open to reveal a young boy, who swiftly vanishes leaving Cane in his place.

Back at the inn, Trent accuses Styles of having staged the disappearance to boost sales of Cane's work. Styles admits it did begin as a hoax, but that events have taken a disturbing turn and the existence of Hobb's End was never part of the plan. Styles returns to the church, where she finds Cane, who shows her the manuscript for his new novel, In the Mouth of Madness. Cane reveals that his stories were dictated to him by a legion of otherworldly beings, and the act of writing them down gave his stories the power to become real. Styles appears hypnotised by Cane's new work, and as the pair begin to kiss, Cane is revealed to be part man, part monster.

Trent discovers the owner of the inn has transformed into a murderous tentacled beast. Seeing that Styles has undergone a similar physical transformation, Trent flees for his safety. As he attempts to drive out of Hobb's End, he finds himself trapped in a nightmarish cycle in which all roads lead back to the town centre. In one last attempt to escape, Trent drives through a rowdy mob, crashing his car and knocking himself unconscious.

Trent awakens in the church, where Cane explains to him that the popularity of his work has liberated an ancient order of monstrous otherworldly beings who will inhabit the Earth, and that Trent is himself nothing more than a work of fiction. Cane demands that Trent deliver his latest manuscript to Arcane Publishing, thus setting the wheels in motion for the destruction of humanity. Cane then proceeds to tear himself open, as if he were a page in a book, opening up a vast chasm from which the unspeakable monsters will come forth. Trent takes the manuscript and flees the beasts, when suddenly he is transported out of Hobb's End and back to 'reality'.

Trent destroys the manuscript and returns to New York where he recounts his experience to an unbelieving Harglow, who denies any knowledge of Styles, claiming he sent Trent on his mission to locate Cane alone. Harglow reveals that Trent delivered the manuscript for In the Mouth of Madness some months before and the book is already at the top of the bestseller list, with a film adaptation to be released imminently. Confused and disturbed by this news, Trent goes to a bookstore where he attacks one of Cane's readers with an axe.

Back in the asylum, Dr Wrenn is sceptical of Trent's claims, assuming them to be the ravings of a madman. The next day Trent wakes up to find his cell door open and the institution abandoned and vandalised. Upon venturing outside he hears news reports that riots have broken out all over the world and widespread violence and murder are rife. He encounters a cinema showing the film version of In the Mouth of Madness, goes inside and takes a seat. As the events he has just lived through unfold on the screen in front of him, Trent breaks into fits of hysterical, deranged laughter.

***

The brainchild of Michael De Luca, future producer of such films as The Social Network (2011) and Fifty Shades of Grey (2015), the screenplay for In the Mouth of Madness was originally written in the late 1980s, but production on the film did not commence until August 1993. John Carpenter had actually been approached to direct around the time of its initial conception, but initially turned the opportunity down. Both Hellbound: Hellraiser II (1988) director Tony Randel and Pet Sematary (1989) helmer Mary Lambert were attached to the project at various stages of development, although neither version came to fruition. Then, like Sutter Cane's manuscript fatefully finding its way to Arcane Publishing, the screenplay would again cross Carpenter's path some years later, and this time he officially signed on as director in December 1992. Filmed in Canada on a budget of around $8 million, In the Mouth of Madness was a modest production, shooting over the course of three months, with Sam Neill, having previously worked with Carpenter on Memoirs of an Invisible Man, taking on the lead role of Trent.

By the time In the Mouth of Madness was finished, De Luca's subsequent screenplay for Freddy's Dead: The Final Nightmare (1991) had already been filmed, while the year of its release, De Luca would also be credited as writer for the first cinematic incarnation of comic book renegade Judge Dredd (1995). Carpenter's film opened in the US in February 1995 to mixed to negative reviews, and while by no means a box office disaster (the film took about $9 million domestic, enough to just about cover its budget), it was something of a commercial disappointment. Failing to convincingly capture the hearts and imaginations of the cinema going public, it promptly disappeared from cinema screens.

In the Mouth of Madness is perhaps best known among Carpenter's fans as the final entry in what the director retrospectively coined his 'Apocalypse Trilogy', an unplanned triptych of films (the first two being *The Thing* and *Prince of Darkness*), which depict the annihilation of human civilisation, brought about by three different malevolent forces. Although the films were created by different writers, produced by different studios, featured no crossovers in the casting or characters, and took distinct stylistic approaches, they are united by a cold, cruel and cynical worldview. These were not straightforward end-of-the-world stories, but insidious and cerebral depictions of the gradual breakdown of interpersonal connection, and eventual destruction of the very idea of personal identity and individuality, whose harbingers of destruction are not simply ghoulish baddies, but incomprehensibly 'other' – not so much inhuman as anti-human. The fact that Carpenter retroactively labelled these films a trilogy in no way diminishes how effectively they function as one cohesive piece, with their creeping progression into bleaker and more abstract territories feeling like something which could feasibly have been planned from the outset.

The triptych kicked off in the vast and uncompromising terrains of Antarctica. *The Thing*, written by screenwriter Bill Lancaster, told the story of a group of American research scientists who find their base camp infiltrated by an unseen (and unseeable?) alien parasite able to assume the shape of any living entity it inhabits. As it becomes increasingly clear that no one can be trusted, tension and paranoia escalate among the group as the men are slowly picked off one by one. The defiantly downbeat conclusion shows just two remaining survivors, the mystery of which of them might be infected left unanswered, but their doomed fate already sealed. A remake of the Christian Nyby/ Howard Hawks film *The Thing From Another World* (1951), itself based on the short story 'Who Goes There?' by John W. Campbell, Carpenter's film was perhaps too bleak in its vision to ever be an immediate commercial success, particularly considering it opened just a few weeks after Steven Spielberg's family-friendly *E.T. The Extra Terrestrial* (1982), whose unthreatening sentimentality offered a far more palatable vision of alien life. It seemed that audiences and critics alike did not want to have their safe Spielbergian bubble burst. At least not so soon anyway.

Far from the mindless gorefest it was initially labelled by doubting critics, the horror at the heart of *The Thing* has lofty existential implications. The alien threat is not a traditional humanoid or an individual entity the audience can discern and get a solid grasp on. More than that, it is incomprehensible, posing a threat to the very sanctity of terrestrial life – as individual, distinct entities with our own minds and souls. The monster is a mysterious and unseeable infection (thus an unnameable 'thing'), only visible via the biological material it infects and transforms. Characters we have begun to know – gruff, boisterous working men with strong wills – are reduced to flat facsimiles of the humans they once were: As one character says, *'If I was an imitation, a perfect imitation, how would you tell if it was me?'* After infection, and prior to their violent attacks on others, people appear unchanged, initially – but they are strange, uncanny versions of their old selves: just a performance of the human individuality which has been annihilated. When 'The Thing' infects, it deletes personal character, and recruits its flesh for abominable ends. It is no respecter of species either – it inhabits and transforms dogs in the same way, and in one of the most memorable sequences in the film we see the slimy, protracted mutation of a canine.

Even after repeat viewings, the downbeat conclusion of *The Thing* still troubles. Such a defiant lack of hope for our protagonists – or the concept of individual character – is disconcerting, not to mention incredibly rare in mainstream Hollywood cinema (it is worth noting that *The Thing* was Carpenter's first major studio production). Still, it is an ending that has the power to become increasingly hopeless the more one ponders it. Part of the film's genius is the way in which it alludes to the end of the world through this small story. On first viewing we are left to believe that either Macready or Childs is likely infected. We worry for them, and we mourn for them – for these characters we have grown to know as individual men with their own personalities, histories and bodies. It is only later that our minds can take the threat to its logical, terrible conclusion: that the billions of individual persons that comprise humanity might soon also be reduced to a slimy, howling pile of flesh.

Produced five years later, *Prince of Darkness* was the only film in the trilogy to be written by Carpenter himself, although he did so under the pseudonym Martin Quatermass, an unambiguous homage to acclaimed British screenwriter Nigel Kneale, a figure who Carpenter had long admired and made frequent allusions to in his films. Kneale's most famed television work *The Quatermass Experiment* (1953), and subsequent TV series and film *Quatermass and the Pit* (1959 and 1967 respectively), about the arrival of a destructive alien lifeform on earth, was itself an obvious influence on *The Thing*. With

Prince of Darkness, Carpenter did not stop with a quick name reference, even going so far as to create a biography for Martin Quatermass for the film's press materials (apparently, 'Prince of Darkness *is his first screenplay, and he assures that all the physical principles used in the story, including the ability of subatomic particles to travel backward in time, are true*').The basic plot of *Prince of Darkness* itself recalls Kneale's acclaimed supernatural drama *The Stone Tape* (1972), in which a group of academics and researchers attempt to utilise scientific practice to determine the roots of a supposed haunting. Aside from fundamental plot crossovers involving otherworldly invasion and mind control, Carpenter's love for all things Kneale-related can be further witnessed in *In the Mouth of Madness* through the name of Cane's hometown, Hobb's End, which was also the name of the fictional London underground station in which *Quatermass and the Pit* was set.

Like *The Thing* before it, *Prince of Darkness* deals with the idea of physical possession which gives way to – or masks – metaphysical transformation, albeit in markedly different ways to its predecessor. Following the death of an elderly priest in downtown Los Angeles, another cleric, Father Loomis, finds himself in possession of an antique journal and a key which unlocks the basement of a decrepit, abandoned church. Upon discovering a large vial of mysterious green liquid in the building's cellar, Loomis invites a physics professor and his students to investigate its origins.The disparate group soon understand that the substance is the very essence of Satan, which begins to spill out, transforming those it touches into zombie-like maniacs, and calling upon an all-powerful anti-God to descend upon the Earth.

As with the alien entity in *The Thing*, the green secretion of *Prince of Darkness* has the power to take over those it comes into contact with, stripping them of their individual personalities and sense of self, leaving them empty vessels used to carry out a malevolent higher plan. While *The Thing* defaults to biomedical science as its theoretical basis (well, biomedical science fiction, at least), this time *religion* is incorporated into the epistemological framework. However, despite making a move away from biological tangibility and towards the spiritual, Carpenter still turned to science for his initial inspiration for the film, explaining that he had been reading up on theoretical physics when he wrote the story.The results saw him graft a horrific dimension onto these theories to create his own unique brand of theological-sci-fi. Carpenter explained, '*Since there is a mirror of anti-matter for every particle of matter, I thought it would be great to have an anti-God, namely a mirror opposite of God that would be totally evil'* (Carpenter in Boulenger, 2003: 201).

In both *The Thing* and *Prince of Darkness*, existential annihilation manifests as a deadly infection. But whereas in *The Thing's* science fiction narrative the infection is a volatile alien life form, in *Prince of Darkness* the contagion comes in the form of the Devil itself, a terrifyingly omnipotent corrupting evil that will infect anyone it comes into contact with. Interestingly, the physical effects on the afflicted are much more immediately visible in *Prince of Darkness*, even though it supposedly functions on the spiritual, rather than biological, plane. Here the infected display stigmata-like wounds, or grotesque skin conditions, with obvious Biblical connotations (the association of Catholic rituals and doctrines with the body, as well as spirit, providing ample opportunities for a breed of divine body-horror). Unlike the consistently downbeat *The Thing, Prince of Darkness* looks set to end on a note of triumph in which the evil is vanquished and good survives to fight another day; however, the final shots indicate something altogether more pessimistic. Carpenter ends with the teasing notion that, even if the satanic threat has been defeated for now, it has not been defeated forever. Once again, as in *The Thing*, the annihilation of humanity is inevitable. It is not a matter of if, but when.

If *The Thing* depicted the end of the world through the cold, clinical gaze of science, and *Prince of Darkness* envisioned the apocalypse from a theological perspective, *In the Mouth of Madness* considers the Armageddon via *art*. The trilogy began with the notion of a literal, physical destructive entity contained within the ice, while the evil of the second instalment manifested as a substance contained within a large glass cylinder. For the finale, Carpenter ditches the notion of a tangible destructive force held prisoner within a physical structure, instead placing the threat within the immateriality of language and ideas. In doing so, the threat is more complicated, more nebulous – and more terrifying. How can something be contained when its cage is composed of concept and thought? In many ways *In the Mouth of Madness* is the most theoretically complex of the trilogy, taking its predecessor's existential preoccupations to new extremes. It directly, even bluntly, questions the entire nature of reality, our knowledge about it, and what it means to exist. And by extension of that, what it means not to exist.

Like the previous two entries, *In the Mouth of Madness* continues to imagine evil as a type of contagion which will bring about the end of the world. But while the infections in *The Thing* and *Prince of Darkness* are transmitted physically, the disease in *In the Mouth of Madness* is passed on through the sharing of stories and ideas, which eventually cause the whole population to go mad. The film begins with the suggestion that madness is on the rise, and by the end – when we see Trent walking through the vandalised asylum – we hear a news broadcast describing a widespread epidemic: *'Every hour, more people are becoming infected being driven to senseless acts of extreme violence… If for any reason you are one of us who hasn't become infected, take shelter immediately. Do not trust any friends or family members.'* The evil unleashed as ideas has contaminated minds, caused mass insanity and prompted the bloody breakdown of social order. Carpenter's concluding vision of the end of the world is a psychotic apocalypse.

While in many ways recalling the urban dystopia of Carpenter's *Escape From New York*, in which the streets of the city have devolved into public arenas of criminality and violence, this broadcast also echoes the news reports littered throughout George Romero's *Night of the Living Dead* (1968), an indicator of the extent to which *In the Mouth of Madness* (and much of Carpenter's filmography) borrows from the zombie genre. In Romero's film, survivors (those still uninfected) are warned against 'ordinary-looking people' who are in a 'kind of trance'. In both *Night of the Living Dead* and *In the Mouth of Madness,* a horrific breakdown of society spreads like a plague, giving rise to a legion of terrifying killers who display violent drives, but little or no free will. Meanwhile, shots of Trent roaming the empty streets at the end of Carpenter's film also call to mind the early scenes of a more recent zombie film, Danny Boyle's *28 Days Later* (2002), in which a virus known as 'rage' turns its victims (not, strictly speaking, zombies) into crazed, unthinking creatures. In each of these films, and zombie cinema generally, the majority of humankind is reduced to mere physical entities, bodies without rational minds – and as such (according to post-Enlightenment, Western values), abject and inhuman. But it is instructive to look at how *In the Mouth of Madness* departs from zombie tropes even as it incorporates them. While Romero's and Boyle's undead are zombies in the classic sense, in that they have had their physical beings inhabited by an infection which has quite literally destroyed their brains and taken over their bodies biologically, the 'zombies' in Carpenter's film are being controlled by an external force (an author) more powerful

Abandoned streets in In the Mouth of Madness *and Danny Boyle's* 28 Days Later

than they are. Quite simply, they have been brainwashed. Or, to put it another way, intellectually contaminated.

In each of the films in the *Apocalypse* Trilogy, the human form has the power to deceive, either through the physical invasion of a transformative alien entity, or the theoretical power of suggestion. Physical deception is a frequent theme throughout Carpenter's cinema, from the unknowable creatures masquerading as children in *Village of the Damned* (1995), to the colonists invaded by a dormant alien race in *Ghosts of Mars* (2001). Characters might often look like us, but appearances lie. As with the classic cinematic zombie, their human bodies may appear alive, but the mind is somewhere else entirely. The deranged killers of *In the Mouth of Madness* are just one breed of many 'zombies' we find in Carpenter's oeuvre, where the loss of individuality and agency is a perennial anxiety. We may not think of Carpenter as a zombie filmmaker (in the way that, say, George Romero is), but his films frequently concern animated bodies without their original minds. But a key difference is that, as compared to traditionally accepted manifestations of the zombie in horror cinema, many of Carpenter's unthinking entities are not actually the 'living dead', as they never died in the first place. Carpenter's zombies are very much alive; the problem is that they are fatally susceptible to the power of suggestion.

As an extension of this, Carpenter's unique brand of zombie finds another incarnation in his later career effort, *The Ward* (2010), whose troubled young protagonist's perceptions are clouded by mental illness, and thus she is robbed of authentic sense of choice. Her agency is further curtailed when she is institutionalised; like Trent she loses any claims to societal command when she is designated as insane. She may not be a zombie in the way they commonly manifest in horror cinema, but she is in essence treated like one by those around her.

Beyond philosophical connotations about the nature of humanity, and notion of bodies without rational minds, the figure of the zombie in horror cinema, with its absence of individuality or self-control, is often discussed in *political* terms. The zombie has frequently been explained as a political allegory, particularly with reference to consumerism (thanks in no small part to Romero's *Dawn of the Dead* (1978) in which his undead instinctively invade a deserted shopping mall). Carpenter's *They Live* (1988) is consistent with the consumerist allegory, imagining a world where aliens employ mind-control techniques to subliminally encourage people to spend their money and submit to mindless capitalist values. *They Live* is not the only film of Carpenter's to express hostility toward corporate and commercial endeavours. *Memoirs of an Invisible Man*, the episode 'Hair' from *Body Bags*, and *Halloween III: Season of the Witch* (1982) (the latter of which he did not direct, but did produce and co-write), all present dystopian views of capitalist ventures which threaten to harm and potentially destroy humanity. This notion of a large company wielding the power to do harm is drolly evident in *In the Mouth of Madness*, with Arkham Publishing determined to flog as many copies of Cane's work as possible, not to mention tie-in merchandise and memorabilia, no matter the cost.

It is therefore only fitting that the opening shots of *In the Mouth of Madness* should depict a factory in which copies of Cane's latest novel roll incessantly off the whirring conveyor belts. Cane's work is part of a production line, his books mechanically churned out to fulfil customer demand. As in *They Live*, Carpenter seems to suggest that the unquestioning, never-ending consumption and blind faith in mass industry will be the death of us all, as if our very destruction is being manufactured. *Christine* also begins with a production line, one in which cars, rather than books, are assembled, again suggesting horror is something which can be thoughtlessly mass produced. One might even argue that Stephen King, upon whose book that film was based, churns out his own novels with workmanlike dependency. From the opening frames of *In the Mouth of Madness*, Carpenter is acknowledging not just the horror of business, but also the business of horror.

Sutter Cane's latest bestseller churns off the printing press

Ultimately, though, *In the Mouth of Madness* resists being read as a simple political allegory which explores the notion of free will within a capitalist society. Those ideas are there, but ultimately the film's rumination on selfhood and agency (or, rather, the impossibility of either) has much grander philosophical implications. When Styles repeatedly cries, '*I'm losing me!*' having read Cane's latest work, she is not expressing an awareness of being a consumerist cog in a capitalist machine, or voicing fears of being brainwashed, but literally doubting her very existence (and later we discover she did not in fact exist, a conundrum when we consider that portions of the film appear to be from her point of view). Existence here is directly related to – and dependent on – agency, individuality, and even (in the Cartesian sense) independent thought. '*I'm losing me*' is a direct, explicit articulation of the profound way that *In the Mouth of Madness* engages with the ideas about the loss of selfhood, not so much as political allegory, but as existential horror. And as nihilist apocalypse.

While *In the Mouth of Madness* is the most philosophically dense and narratively disorientating of the *Apocalypse* Trilogy, its conclusion presents the most concrete depiction of the end of days in the series. As Trent emerges from the institution, it is clear that Cane's unholy beasts have already gotten their slimy tentacles on most of the population, and Trent now stands as one of the last remaining humans in a barren landscape which feels like an empty soundstage, devoid of fellow actors. Trent enters the cinema at the film's cruelly humorous denouément, and the seats around him remain empty (a bitter irony given the film's real life failure to attract much of an audience). Trent is truly alone, and left to deal with the overwhelming notion that he never really existed in the first place, but was merely a product of another man's imagination. Orrin Grey neatly summarises how this ontological disorientation distinguishes *In the Mouth of Madness* from the other films in Carpenter's trilogy in his article 'Cosmic Horror in John Carpenter's *Apocalypse* Trilogy', writing: '*While* The Thing *threatened the annihilation of the human species, and* Prince of Darkness *posited an illogical universe in which god was malevolent,* In the Mouth of Madness *paints a picture of a world in which there is no objective reality at all*' (Grey, 2011). The term 'cosmic horror' is itself very useful for understanding the kind of terror that Carpenter depicts: it is the distinctly Lovecraftian terror that humankind experiences when faced with the yawning chasm of nothingness beneath the façade of the universe. These ideas will be explored further in the next chapter.

Much like the uncontainable satanic ooze in *Prince of Darkness*, themes of ancient evils and monstrous invasion spill out across the rest of John Carpenter's filmography, with many of the key concepts found in *In the Mouth of Madness* evocative of his past work. The resurgence of ancient evil is not something confined only to his three depictions of the Armageddon, it can also be witnessed in *The Fog*, in which a mysterious mist brings forth the vengeful spirits of long-deceased mariners to an unsuspecting coastal town. *The Fog* also depicts the discovery of an ancient journal which provides answers to the bizarre events taking place, much like the diary that Father Loomis comes into possession of in *Prince of Darkness*, and of course the fundamental motif of the written word as key to unlocking the secrets of the supernatural in *In the Mouth of Madness.*

As previously mentioned, Carpenter's eschatological preoccupations can be seen in his dystopian vision of a corrupt future, *Escape from New York*. Meanwhile, the fatalistic notion that evil can never truly be destroyed or overcome is evident at the conclusion of *Halloween*, when the supposedly dead Michael Myers proves indestructible, despite being shot multiple times. Similarly, *Christine* ends on another note of pessimism, in which the titular car, having been crushed to a seemingly harmless pulp, is seen moving as though beginning the process of physical regeneration. There is no time to relax, Carpenter is telling his audience, there is life in the old girl yet.

But while *In the Mouth of Madness* serves as both a logical conceptual conclusion to Carpenter's *Apocalypse* Trilogy, and an extension of many themes explored throughout his career, stylistically it presents a significant departure from the films (particularly the horror ones) that had come before. This aesthetic shift reflects the progression of the themes he has explored throughout the trilogy, with his final instalment taking things to the next (metaphysical) level. To effectively convey his new ideas, a new cinematic language is needed. Thematically, *In the Mouth of Madness* might present itself as classic Carpenter, but stylistically it can often feel disorientingly unfamiliar.

As the pages of Cane's latest work systematically roll off the conveyer belts, one of the film's most immediately apparent stylistic differences is the music, which sees Carpenter renounce his typically foreboding electronic melodies, in favour of a healthy dose of rock and roll. The heavy metal guitar riff, which bears more than a passing resemblance to Metallica's 'Enter Sandman' (a possible hint to the surrealist nightmare we are about to embark upon?), is a prime indicator that Carpenter is forgoing subtlety this time around. This is the end of the world, there is no time to ease you gently into it. Carpenter's signature synths do feature in the sonic textures of *In the Mouth of Madness*, although his score this time around is notably less rhythmic than we have come to expect, lacking in discernible themes or hooks (so intrinsic to the mood of previous films such as *Halloween* or *Prince of Darkness*), building instead on ambient atmosphere, with background sounds of distant screams, moans and groans adding an almost subliminal sense of unease and disquiet to proceedings.

The dynamic energy of the film's opening guitar riff is aptly (if perhaps surprisingly) matched by a similarly punchy succession of edits. As the credits roll over the bustling printing press in full swing, Carpenter employs a succession of quick cuts and close-ups, creating a feverish sense of urgency, poles apart from, say, the protracted opening shots of *The Fog*, or the almost infuriatingly long titles of *Prince of Darkness*. If Carpenter's films are known for taking their time, and for the measured build-up of tension and mood, just seconds into *In the Mouth of Madness* it is clear that we are in markedly different territory. Carpenter does not allow the viewer the luxury of time in which to slowly acquaint themselves with his new world vision, instead he bursts in all guns blazing.

Such atypical aesthetic choices are not confined to the opening credits, but permeate the visual language of the entire film. As with the anomalous aural landscape, Carpenter surprises by largely abandoning his penchant for long takes and uninterrupted tracking shots. Several sequences employ uncharacteristic rapid-fire montage techniques (namely in dream sequences or moments in which characters are witness to flash forwards or flashbacks of the mounting horrors) designed to disorientate and unsettle. While Carpenter's previous horror films had often utilised empty space and periods of extended silence as a means of generating unease, *In the Mouth of Madness* forgoes such subtleties in favour of more immediate scares. Unlike the slow burn, often languid, pacing we had come to expect, *In the Mouth of Madness* is fast and furious – Carpenter for the MTV generation. Yet such a stylistic shift is not indicative of a dilution of Carpenter's directorial voice, nor a dumbing down in his approach (as Ms. Kael might have had us believe), but rather the desire (or need) to find a new language with which to tell a very different story. The rapid edits, and the atypical skewed camera angles are symptomatic of Trent's increasingly fractured psyche, while the playful use of dream sequences and visual repetition (something which we will return to later in the book) are indicators that the increasingly surreal events may well be unfolding in the twisted mind of Sutter Cane. We are operating on a more subjective level than Carpenter has done so previously, and his stylistic approach mirrors the sense of intangibility which comes with it. As John Carpenter said himself when discussing the film, '*I am doing some things that I haven't done before – a lot of abstract and subliminal cuts, because this is a movie about reality not being what we think it is*' (Carpenter in Rowe, 1995).

However, despite this desire to try out new techniques, Carpenter does not abandon all of his aesthetic trademarks entirely, proudly maintaining one which has routinely employed since *Assault on Precinct 13* – anamorphic widescreen. Very much a child of the 1950s, Carpenter has named 1953 (the year in which CinemaScope was launched) as the exact moment in which his love of cinema was first ignited. His continued use of Panavision (the format successor of CinemaScope) throughout his career acknowledges the impact of those formative cinematic experiences in which he first grasped the full scope and spectacle of the big screen. With his fondness for widescreen very much informed by his early trips to the movies, and his storytelling techniques so often indebted to classical Hollywood, the cinema of Carpenter has often felt like a throwback to a different time, and this fondness for nostalgia makes the flashy, 'modern' techniques of *In the Mouth of Madness* all the more notable – the frame may be the same, but the picture inside is quite different.

According to Le Blanc and Odell, 'Carpenter brings modern technology and innovation to classical Hollywood techniques' (Le Blanc and Odell, 2011: 18), and nowhere is this innovation more apparent than in *In the Mouth of Madness*, which is a prime example of how Carpenter's visual language is there to serve and enhance the story, and not the other way around. Even if that means a radical overhaul of his fundamental approach.

Chapter 3: 'All those horrible, slimy things'

Has there ever been a writer whose work more accurately defines the term 'unfilmable' than H.P. Lovecraft? With his science-fiction infused horror tales of unspeakable, slimy abominations from other realms, Lovecraft crafted a literary universe so entirely distinctive and so perversely unfathomable as to render most cinematic adaptations almost futile. Lovecraft's dense prose was grotesquely descriptive yet infuriatingly vague at the same time, allowing his readers a fleeting glimpse into the horrors of his otherworldly creations without ever truly letting them know what they were witness to. The old cliché that it is what we do *not* see that remains the most frightening might be most apt in the case of Lovecraft; after all, how can we even begin to comprehend the monstrosities he describes, which are so far removed from the realms of human understanding as to become almost entirely abstract?

Lovecraft's particular worldview also makes adapting his work a tricky proposition for cinema (certainly for any filmmaker looking to make popular and profitable horror fare). Lovecraft's attitude towards the universe (and humanity's place within it) is so singularly nihilistic that it constitutes its own philosophical-literary construct: Cosmicism. With *In the Mouth of Madness*, Carpenter is among the few filmmakers who has seriously attempted to present cosmicism in cinematic terms: to film the unknowable, the unspeakable, the unseeable. In the laws of Lovecraft's cosmic universe, there is no one God or divine presence, and humanity is a mere side note in the epic vastness of space and time. The very incomprehensibility of Lovecraft's horrors undermines humanist faith in our powers of perception and understanding – they are irredeemably other because we are unable to grasp them with our puny human minds. Such rampant misanthropy positioned humans as having no more significance than insects, or even bacteria, crawling on the surface of the Earth, under constant threat of extermination from more powerful, more advanced lifeforms. We may consider *In the Mouth of Madness* not only an attempt to respectfully bring forth Lovecraft's 'horrible slimy things' to the screen, but also to render the unspeakable metaphysical horrors of his universe and the futility of humanity's place within it. And thus it is time to explore the tentacular entanglements between Carpenter and Lovecraft in more depth, and to chart the horrific results of the director's engagement with Lovecraft's supposedly unfilmable fiction.

If his *Apocalypse* Trilogy proves anything, it is that John Carpenter has a propensity for pessimism – as already alluded to, there is no real sense that any human will survive the Carpenterian apocalypse and achieve salvation. It is this disposition which makes Carpenter and Lovecraft such perfect bedfellows, and demonstrates why Carpenter would be attracted to Lovecraftian philosophy (and indeed to De Luca's screenplay) to provide the conceptual backbone for the final instalment of his cinematic Armageddon. But before we look at the various ways in which *In the Mouth of Madness* utilises and updates Lovecraftian themes, and the ways in which it makes both direct and indirect references to the author's prose throughout, perhaps it is useful to explore some of the adaptations which have come before.

Many filmmakers have tried to bring Lovecraft's stories to the big screen, but while there have been a handful of interesting attempts, the majority of adaptations fall short of capturing Lovecraft's singular vision in a truly satisfactory way; not simply the incomprehensible creatures and the weird narratives, but the devastating, pessimistic nihilism of the Lovecraftian universe. Some of the most effective examples of Lovecraft-inspired cinema take his work as a loose blueprint, a mere starting point to create something else entirely. Stuart Gordon's *Re-Animator* (1985) uses the foundations of Lovecraft's story, 'Herbert West – Re-Animator', but inverts it to create a raucous splatter comedy that substitutes the dread and unease of the original text with a liberal dose of knockabout humour and gloopy gore effects. Ultimately, Gordon's stylistic liberties show a perverse kind of respect for Lovecraft's craft: by choosing not to make a 'loyal' adaptation, he acknowledges the near-impossibility of representing the complexity of Lovecraft's work onscreen (further demonstrated in the similarly playful approach employed in his Lovecraft-inspired shocker *From Beyond* (1986)). Brian Yuzna's continuation of the Herbert West mythos, *Bride of Re-Animator* (1989), was an equally mischievous mash-up of the original texts, infusing Lovecraftian themes with an affectionate homage to the iconic Universal monster movies of the 1940s. Such tongue in cheek exercises serve as heartfelt love letters to a legend, the attempts of Lovecraft admirers to say thank you, even if they fundamentally (and deliberately) fail to capture the ever-intangible essence and inherent solemnity of his written work.

When considering Lovecraft on film, it is the more 'faithful' adaptations which frequently prove more problematic. One of the first films to proudly place Lovecraft's name at the forefront was the Roger Corman-produced *The Dunwich Horror* (1970), although the film was only moderately successful, failing to bring forth a glut of Lovecraft adaptations in its wake, the way in which Corman's *House of Usher* (1960) had done for fellow horror scribe Edgar Allan Poe a decade before. *Necronomicon* (1993) was an interesting, if uneven, anthology film which riffed on a variety of Lovecraftian concepts, and featured fairly literal adaptations of two of his stories, 'Cool Air' and 'The Whisper in Darkness', the latter of which was directed by *Bride of Re-Animator*'s Brian Yuzna, who also directed the film's wraparound story. Less well regarded, Jean-Paul Ouellette's low-budget *The Unnamable* (1988) unsuccessfully updated Lovecraft's original tale to the modern day, and followed a gang of unfortunate teens who are picked off one by one by a grotesque monster after deciding to spend the night in a supposedly haunted house. Fresh from the successes of *Re-Animator* and *From Beyond*, Stuart Gordon returned in subsequent decades with further adaptations of his master's tales, this time eschewing the broad comic tones of his previous works in an attempt to capture a more robust portrait of Lovecraft on screen. *Castle Freak* (1995) was a schlocky, sporadically effective, retelling of Lovecraft's short story 'The Outsider', about a beast kept hidden in the cellar of a vast mansion, while *Dagon* (2001) was a faithful retelling of 'The Shadow over Innsmouth', which, though reasonably well received by some Lovecraft enthusiasts, failed to make much of an impact elsewhere. While some of these examples are more effective than others, each is undone by the desire to simply transpose, rather than adapt, Lovecraft's material for the screen. Lovecraft's stories were structurally complex and thematically introspective, qualities that do not make for accessible popular cinema. A literal replication of Lovecraft's stories on screen might prove of interest to pre-existing fans (those bringing with them a rigorous understanding of Lovecraftian philosophies), but for audiences unfamiliar with the reference material, finding a way in can prove rather difficult. Where most cinematic translations of Lovecraft's work fail, but *In the Mouth of Madness* triumphs, is in the ability to distinguish the material from its literary source, retaining the essence of what defines Lovecraft, yet reposition it within an original cinematic landscape which exists on its own terms.

Another reason that Lovecraft's work has proven so consistently difficult to translate into a visual medium is the brevity of his character development and lack of investment in relatable human experience. It could be argued that no one was ever drawn to his work for the rich characters or compelling emotional arcs. Lovecraft was not a writer concerned with the complex emotional register of characters (other than that of fear), nor did he have any interest in detailing their interpersonal relations, be it in the form of friendship, or, god forbid, romantic or sexual encounters. Furthermore, Lovecraft rarely featured female characters in his stories, and when he did they were never the main protagonist. In his memoir *On Writing*, Stephen King said that whilst '*Lovecraft was a genius when it comes to writing tales of the macabre*' (King 2000: 143) he was damning about his dialogue, calling it '*terrible (...) stilted and lifeless*' (ibid.). He must have known it, King surmises, because '*in the millions of words of fiction he wrote, fewer than five thousand are dialogue*' (ibid.). King goes on to explain how Lovecraft was a snob and a loner (not to mention a racist), his awkward dialogue unarguably the product of a man not accustomed to the art of everyday conversation, and without any real interest or empathy for other people. However, if Lovecraft's dialogue was distinctly uncompelling, then his prose was the exact opposite, rich and complex, verging on the wilfully opaque, as this extract from 'At the Mountains of Madness' demonstrates:

> The leathery, undeteriorative, and almost indestructible quality was an inherent attribute of The Thing's form of organisation, and pertained to some paleogean cycle of invertebrate evolution utterly beyond our powers of speculation. (Lovecraft, 1936)

Lovecraft's lexis is a fitting match for the heady complexities of his cosmic theories, but whilst his fertile vocabulary makes his work so fascinating (and rewarding) on the page, it resists cinematic adaptation. His writing was such that it almost actively defies visual interpretation – as though Lovecraft deliberately set out to sabotage any filmmakers' efforts. In some of his earlier critical writing Lovecraft discussed film in a positive manner, expressing a particular affection for the work of Charlie Chaplin. However, it seems he quickly became tired of the medium, ultimately labelling it as crude and unsophisticated, incapable of representing his incomprehensible creations which, by their very nature, resisted the visual directness cinema possesses as a medium. His distaste for cinema was at its peak when he declared in a letter to the poet Richard Morse that he would '*never permit anything bearing my signature to be banalised and vulgarised into the flat infantile twaddle which passes for horror tales amongst radio and cinema audiences*' (Lovecraft to Morse, 1933).

Thank God he never lived to see *The Unnamable*.

When considering some of the less successful adaptations of his work, it is hard to resolutely dismiss Lovecraft's assertion that cinema has banalising effects. What each of those aforementioned 'literal' adaptations of Lovecraft's work struggled to evoke is that palpable and pervasive (but always 'unspeakable') sense of absolute horror that is so intrinsic to his work. Guillermo del Toro, a long-standing admirer of Lovecraft's work, who has famously tried to get a big budget adaptation of 'At the Mountains of Madness' off the ground on numerous occasions, supported this claim when he said:

> It is not a matter of how big the creature is, or how slimy, or how many tentacles pop out or not. If you do a Lovecraft story or a movie, and you do not give a sense of cosmology and a sense of otherness that is absolutely devastating, then it's not a Lovecraft movie. (Del Toro in Migliore and Strysik, 2006: 210)

As proven by Stuart Gordon's *Re-Animator*, this sense of otherness, and the potent power of Lovecraft's work is perhaps better illustrated in those films that simply borrow an idea or two from his stories and embed them within their own unique mythology, to create something anew rather than try to match the master. Del Toro himself did this in *Hellboy* (2004), a superhero action blockbuster which boasted some familiar tentacled monsters, and also in *Pacific Rim* (2013), which again flirted with several Lovecraftian concepts. Elsewhere the writer's influence can be traced in the creature design of Ridley Scott's atmospheric slice of cosmic horror *Alien* (1979), in the subterranean caverns of Mariano Baino's *Dark Waters* (1993), or in the references to the Necronomicon (whether explicit or merely implied) found in both Sam Raimi's *The Evil Dead* (1981) and Lucio Fulci's *The Beyond* (1981).

In the Mouth of Madness falls very much into the latter category of films which take Lovecraftian themes as the raw ingredients for an original work. But rather than simply throwing in a handful of references, before stepping aside from an attempt to produce a thoroughly Lovecraftian experience, De Luca's script resolutely commits to the enterprise. He borrows from Lovecraft in quite literal ways (slimy, tentacled creatures), but also – as del Toro insists a 'Lovecraft movie' should – he seeks to fully capture the devastatingly pessimistic essence of the writer's work, and the true sense of 'otherness' his horror conveys, and depends on. And so, whilst it is not an adaptation of one specific story, *In the Mouth of Madness* ends up arguably the most faithful Lovecraft adaptation there ever (or rather never) was.

There are many explicit allusions to Lovecraft's work littered throughout *In the Mouth of Madness* (the names of characters and places, for example), which turns the film into a playful game of 'spot the Lovecraft reference'. These references are not just reminders that the author's philosophy serves as the fundamental key to unlocking the mysteries of the film, but also attest to De Luca's own very personal affection for the writer, a fondness shared also by Carpenter who has frequently expressed his admiration for Lovecraft. Carpenter once said, '*Lovecraft brings compelling visions of nightmarish fear, invisible worlds and the demons of the unconscious. If one author truly represents the very best in American literary horror, it is HP Lovecraft*' (Carpenter in Roland, 2014).

The frequent references to the writer's stories in *In the Mouth of Madness* are more than just a surface nod or fanboy homage, also signalling the importance of Lovecraft's work as part of this cinematic universe. Such references begin with the film's title itself, a composite of two Lovecraft stories: 'At the Mountains of Madness' and 'The Shadow over Innsmouth'. As with most of Carpenter's films, the film is also known under the longer title *John Carpenter's In the Mouth of Madness*. This claim of ownership on one hand positions Carpenter as the author of this text (even though it was not actually written by him), making it clear that this is above all else his tale – not Lovecraft's, nor screenwriter De Luca's. However, it can also be read as though Carpenter is himself in the mouth – 'John Carpenter *is* In the Mouth of Madness' – swallowed by Lovecraft, consumed by his world and in thrall to his horrors.

Over the course of the film we learn the titles for seven of Sutter Cane's fictional novels, which themselves sound as if they could have spilled out of Lovecraft's own pen. In addition to the titular tale, Cane's novel 'The Thing in The Basement' is a direct descendant of Lovecraft's 'The Thing on the Doorstep', 'The Whisperer of the Dark' is a slight variation on 'The Whisperer in Darkness'; 'Haunter Out of Time' serves as a mash up of two Lovecraft tales, 'The Haunter of the Dark' and 'The Shadow Out of Time',

A selection of Cane's novels

while Cane's monstrously successful book 'The Hobb's End Horror' is reminiscent of one of Lovecraft's most popular stories 'The Dunwich Horror'. Although not making direct reference to specific tales, both Cane's 'The Feeding' and 'The Breathing Tunnel' betray a Lovecraftian sensibility, particularly the latter with its evocation of a living, pulsating organic structure.

Not only does De Luca's script borrow from the titles of Lovecraft's stories, but on several occasions lifts passages directly from his works to form part of Cane's writing. Cane quite literally becomes a fictionalised version of Lovecraft, writing with the very same words. In the scene when Trent peers into the black void that Cane has torn open within his physical self, Styles reads aloud the following extract from Cane's manuscript: *'Trent stood at the edge of the rift, stared into the illimitable gulf of the unknown, the Stygian world yawning blackly beyond.'*

The language and texture of the syntax is clearly inspired by Lovecraft, but even more than a mere *homage*, this passage recalls a line from 'The Rats in the Walls', in which our narrator describe how:

I saw my old black cat dart past me like a winged Egyptian god, straight into the illimitable gulf of the unknown. (Lovecraft, 1924)

When Trent and Styles approach the Byzantine Church for the first time, Trent, treating Cane's text as though it were the town's official tourist guidebook, reads an excerpt from 'The Hobb's End Horror' describing the temple: *'This place had once been the seat of an evil older than mankind and wider than the known universe, as a place of pain and suffering beyond human understanding.'*

This is once again a deliberate reference to Lovecraft's writing, borrowing this time from 'The Haunter of the Dark', in which the central character becomes similarly fascinated by a mysterious old church in which *'a monstrous evil had once dwelt'* (Lovecraft, 1936). Elsewhere, during the earlier scene when Trent and Styles arrive at the Pickman Hotel, Styles looks anxiously towards the greenhouse, and, paraphrasing from one of Cane's novels, explains: *'This is empty now. It used to be filled with strange growing things... remember? One night, the townspeople saw something moving in here... something enormous, with arms like snakes.'*

Such mention of these 'strange growing things' recalls Lovecraft's 'The Colour Out of Space', in which a crashed meteor slowly transforms a small farm in Arkham. As Lovecraft describes, *'Strangeness had come into everything growing now'* (Lovecraft, 1927). Although less direct than the previous references, it again demonstrates the ways in which the ghosts of his prose haunt almost every scene in the film. Trent and Styles may have stumbled upon Hobb's End, but they might as well be in Arkham (even the name of Cane's New York publishing house, Arcane, bears more than passing resemblance to Lovecraft's fictional town). In case anyone had thus far missed the Lovecraftian connections, Carpenter makes sure to check the pair into the Pickman Hotel, a direct nod to Lovecraft's story 'Pickman's Model', about a painter famous for creating grotesque and horrific works of art. And sure enough, on the wall of the reception of the Pickman Hotel is a painting, whose image changes of its own accord, becoming more grotesque as the film goes on, much like the haunted painting at the beginning of Nicolas Roeg's *The Witches* (1990).

In the Mouth of Madness was not the first time that Carpenter's work made explicit reference to Lovecraft. *The Thing* took inspiration from 'At the Mountains of Madness', which told the story of a group of scientists who travel to the Antarctic on a research expedition, only to unearth an ancient shape-shifting alien civilisation. Such similarities do not end with the plotline; the film's practical effects feature enough slimy appendages and unspeakable monsters to make Lovecraft proud. *The Fog* too has a very Lovecraftian sensibility, with its glowing mists and antique prophetic almanac, and even features a brief moment when we hear mention of '*Whately Point and Arkham Reef*' on a radio broadcast (Whately being a name Lovecraft gave to several of his characters). Such fleeting references are indicative not just of an innate affection for Lovecraft, but also invite us to explore the ways Carpenter might be more intimately influenced by Lovecraft, signalling a deeper affinity with the writer's nihilistic preoccupations. While De Luca's original script bore enough Carpenterian traits to make it fit comfortably alongside the director's existing work, one might assume that Carpenter was most drawn to it for its Lovecraftian qualities, offering him the chance, at last, to make a full-blown Lovecraft movie. Not only did the script offer a compelling end to his soon to be *Apocalypse* Trilogy, but also provided the logical conclusion to a career spent in admiration of Lovecraft. As Carpenter himself said:

> I was drawn to the fact that it was really Lovecraft. It wasn't 'by day', but it was really Lovecraft. I just thought 'that's great'. Because there really hasn't been a good Lovecraft movie… Mike DeLuca wrote the screenplay, and there's a lot of love in it for Lovecraft, and for old horror and science fiction movies. So I'm happy we did it. (Carpenter in Seibold, 2013)

As mentioned previously, central to a complete understanding of Lovecraft's work, and in turn an understanding of Carpenter's film, are his theories of cosmicism and the position humankind occupies in the wider, unknown reaches of the galaxy. Stemming from Lovecraft's disdain for religion, his fictional philosophies are not so much atheist in their stance as they are polytheist, with his frequent mention of 'Gods' contributing to the overriding notion being that humans are infinitesimal and fundamentally unable to comprehend the true scale of the universe. As such, accepted modes of science and rational thought are rendered obsolete.

Lovecraft's distrust in traditional religious models may initially seem at odds with the theological leanings of Carpenter's *Prince of Darkness*, although one of the characters in that film, a professor of physics, succinctly articulates a worldview that is consistent with Lovecraft's cosmicism:

> From Job's friends insisting that the good are rewarded and the wicked punished, to the scientists of the 1930s proving to their horror a theorem that not everything can be proved, we've sought to impose order on the universe. But we have discovered

something very surprising. While order does exist in the universe, it is not at all what we had in mind.

With these words, Carpenter's physicist suggests that the universe is quite simply too large for humankind to adhere to simplistic notions of order and religion, countering the kind of exceptionalism that religion attributes to humans, deducing that they are, and always have been, insignificant.

Cosmicism denies the existence of free will for humans, or any sense of a spiritual plane: only cold, hard (and uncaring) material universe exists. Lovecraft's philosophy ultimately prompts a general indifference toward humanity (and the flimsy structures from which it derives meaning), and this has major implications for his approach to fiction. It does not allow much room for emotion to register in Lovecraft's work, which explains why his characters and dialogue are often perceived as flat and lifeless. If humans are essentially insignificant (and their way of perceiving and interpreting the universe so phoney), why pretend their emotional responses are of any importance? Lovecraft's lack of interest in human feeling, and furthermore his active disdain for the triviality of individual ego, is epitomised in a letter written in 1927 to Farnsworth Wright, editor of pulp magazine Weird Tales, in which the writer explained, 'All my tales are based on the fundamental premise that common human laws and interests and emotions have no validity or significance in the vast cosmos at large' (Lovecraft to Wright, 1927).

And thus, we have another problem for Lovecraftian cinema, since audiences (of popular film at least) demand characters that they can identify with, root for, or simply just like. The principal focus of In the Mouth of Madness, as with Lovecraft's fiction, concerns ideas rather than character. But, nonetheless, and thanks in no small part to Sam Neill's irresistibly sardonic performance, Trent is a compelling protagonist, a human lens through which the audience navigates the twists and folds of the film's cerebral games. The audience experiences the cosmic terror with him, and Carpenter treats Trent's anxieties, disorientation and fear with empathy rather than indifference or sadism. This is perhaps what most convincingly separates In the Mouth of Madness from those less successful adaptations which had come before – empathy. Trent is a fully realised character (capable of fear and desire, joy and sadness), the likes of which Lovecraft was incapable (or simply unwilling) of producing. More specifically, Trent bears one particular quality that Lovecraft's characters never do – a sense of humour. Wisecracking his way through the film, Trent's sarcastic banter acts as a barrier by which he can distance himself from the horrors around him, whilst giving audiences a reason to understand and be entertained by him. Through his emotional range and (mostly) relatable reactions toward his increasingly hopeless situation, Trent is distinctly un-Lovecraftian, and in being thus, makes it possible for a newcomer to engage with both the immediate narrative and the wider implications of the film's complex philosophy.

Interestingly, while the film takes time to explore Trent's metaphysical anguish and chart his emotional reactions to the horrors unfolding around him, it is far less preoccupied with depicting his, or indeed anyone else's, physical pain. Unlike much of horror cinema, which relishes in the masochistic pleasures of seeing the body endure invasive acts of violence, here Trent's mental suffering proves to be the chief concern. We do encounter the odd maimed child or severed appendage along the way, but these moments are mere seasoning for the bigger horrors at hand. The climactic moments of Trent laughing maniacally in the movie theatre could therefore be seen as equivalent to a similar character in another horror film screaming in physical agony. Such lack of interest in bodily discomfort is consistent with Lovecraft's cosmic horror, which, in addition to being dismissive of human emotion, is similarly uninterested in the material human body. In his work physical pain and death are but passing agonies, and the source of genuine horror is the terrifying realisation that the world is not as we comprehend it, that there is an alternate cosmic law beyond our realm of understanding, and our immediate experiences and perceptions are, ultimately, illusory. In his essay, 'Supernatural Horror in Literature', Lovecraft articulated his concepts about the wider horrors of the universe and the desire to look beyond the basic notions of humankind.

A certain atmosphere of breathless and unexplainable dread of outer, unknown forces must be present; and there must be a hint, expressed with a seriousness and portentousness becoming its subject, of that most terrible conception of the human brain – a malign and particular suspension or defeat of those fixed laws of Nature which are our only safeguard against the assaults of chaos and the daemons of unplumbed space. (Lovecraft, 1927)

The 'unexplainable dread' which Lovecraft describes, not to mention the sense of portentousness and chaos, are all present in Carpenter's film; they are simply made more palatable for the casual viewer thanks to the addition of, say, sympathetic protagonists or a knowing streak of humour. In this sense, Carpenter authentically brings Lovecraftian philosophy to the big screen, but softens some of the writer's more alienating narrative qualities.

Yet, while *In the Mouth of Madness* goes to great lengths to present a more accessible interpretation of cosmicism, there are key Lovecraftian tropes which are transposed to the screen with stricter reverence – most notably Lovecraft's obsession with the written word, and the power it can harbour. The power of the written word is a potent plot device in Lovecraft's stories, most obviously manifesting in the form of the Necronomicon, a macabre compendium that featured in a number of his stories. In truly Lovecraftian fashion, literature and language form the foundations for the horrors we witness over the course of Carpenter's film, with words acting as the metaphorical keys to unlocking the evils which spill out onto the frame.

The pages of Sutter Cane's new novel contain the means to bring forth the unspeakable entities of other worlds – the 'old ones', as Lovecraft might refer to them. Cane's manuscript is his Necronomicon, the key to unlocking the mysteries of the universe and ultimately destroying humankind. As with Lovecraft, the words contained within his fantastical pages are the most powerful objects at his disposal. Words, quite literally, have the capacity to annihilate humanity. According to the iconic quote attributed to William S. Burroughs, *'Language is a virus from outer space'*, a rather fitting sentiment when considered in relation to Cane's universe. Cane claims that he used to believe his work was pure fiction, the product of an active imagination, but has since realised that 'they' were telling him what to write all along. If language is a virus, then Cane is Patient Zero, the first to be contaminated and the one to spread this deadly plague throughout the world.

The concept of a fêted artwork with the power to end the world was later explored again by Carpenter in his *Masters of Horror* episode 'Cigarette Burns' (2005), only this time that power is initially wrought through image rather than language. In the episode, a young woman is tasked with tracking down the only existing print of an infamous film named 'La Fin Absolue du Monde' (i.e. The Absolute End of the World) for an eccentric movie collector. Understood to provoke psychotic and violent reactions among those who view it, the film has not been seen for years, and all those who were involved in its production are dead. As with literature in *In the Mouth of Madness*, 'Cigarette Burns' imagines a world in which cinema can be so potent it can kill. In both films, one text has the viral power to infect its consumer and bring about the end of everything. In Carpenter's world, there is nothing (not even aliens in the ice or evil green goo) more powerful and potent than art.

One might also think of *The King in Yellow*, a collection of short stories by Robert W. Chambers first published in 1895. The collection, reported to have been a direct influence on Lovecraft, features within it a fictional play, itself named 'The King in Yellow'. This play is said to be so powerful that, much like Cane's work or 'La Fin Absolue Du Monde', it will drive insane anyone who should read it or see it performed. As with the cosmic horrors of Lovecraft, this play exposes the incomprehensible and terrifying realities of the wider universe, which prove too much for the human mind to process.

Structurally, *In the Mouth of Madness* takes inspiration from Lovecraft's story 'The Case of Charles Dexter Ward', which begins and ends in an asylum, with the majority of the tale spent unearthing the strange events that led to the alleged insanity of its titular character. Both narratives present us with a person of questionable mental health, a potentially unreliable first person narrator who will serve as our guide through these tales. In many of Lovecraft's stories, his central characters appear to sink deeper and deeper into dementia, leaving the reader unsure of whether the events on the page are real or simply the delusional ravings of a lunatic. *In the Mouth of Madness* leaves us with a similar feeling. Recalling the subjective narratives of *The Cabinet of Dr Caligari* (1920) or *Invasion of the Body Snatchers* (1956), both of which imply their central heroes might not be of sound mind, we are openly invited to speculate whether the whole film might have simply existed within Trent's unstable psyche, particularly as he laughs maniacally at the film's conclusion. Meanwhile, Carpenter also utilises another Lovecraftian archetype, that of the scholar driven mad by forbidden knowledge. Both Trent and Cane represent variations on this theme, two reasonable, intelligent men slowly understanding that they are not in control of their destinies, but that destiny is controlling them.

In spite of its cosmological and existential preoccupations, arguably the most enduring elements of Lovecraftian literature are the monsters themselves. At one point during *In the Mouth of Madness*, after Trent has begun to read Cane's work, he argues that all his novels boil down to the same thing, '*Slimy things in the dark, people go mad, they turn into monsters*'. This is actually a fairly accurate description of Lovecraft's work too. In fact, Trent's summation functions almost as a humorous self-contained haiku on the literary tropes of Lovecraft. Among Lovecraft's countless descriptions of his unearthly creations, perhaps the most famous comes during 'At the Mountains of Madness', in which he describes the appearance of his infamous shoggoth:

> It was a terrible, indescribable thing vaster than any subway train — a shapeless congeries of protoplasmic bubbles, faintly self-luminous, and with myriads of temporary eyes forming and un-forming as pustules of greenish light all over the tunnel-filling front that bore down upon us, crushing the frantic penguins and slithering over the glistening floor that it and its kind had swept so evilly free of all litter. (Lovecraft, 1936)

Lovecraft's genius was to be at once detailed yet somehow nebulous. If ten readers were asked to draw the shoggoth as they imagined it to look, it is likely that each drawing would be wildly different. Lovecraft keeps his beasts in the realm of the intangible, always mysterious and impossible to describe using the limited vocabulary that we, as mere mortals, have at our disposal. It is almost as though to be told exactly what one of these Gods truly looked like would be too much for humankind to comprehend. And there lies another fundamental problem with bringing Lovecraft to the screen: how can these unspeakables manifest physically in a way as to satisfy the imaginations of Lovecraft's devoted readers? To not show them at all would seem the obvious solution, although that would invariably feel like a cop out. Carpenter tries to have it both ways, not shying away from putting the beasts up on the screen, but showing us just enough that they still retain a cool air of mystery – the cinematic equivalent of Lovecraft's literary vaguery. When Trent makes his escape from Hobb's End, running through the passageway (the breathing tunnel?) and away from the army of cosmological cephalopods pursuing him, Carpenter gives us flashes of the unimaginable horrors that are chasing him: a slimy, gaping mouth here, a grotesque claw there. We get to see enough that we can recognise these creatures as nothing other than Lovecraftian (in fact, one of The Things seems to fit the description of Lovecraft's most famous monster Cthulhu), but not so much that we can fully grasp their abstract physiologies. One of the pleasures of this digital age is the ability to pause individual shots, taking the time to truly admire the beasts in all their monstrous glory.

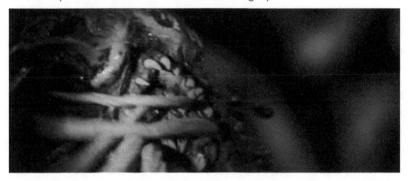

A glimpse at one of Cane's monsters

Still, the revelation of the creatures was not deemed a success by everyone, with many of the film's detractors claiming that Carpenter's decision to let the slimy things run riot was a mistake. Even Fangoria magazine, who had covered the film extensively in the run up to its release come out with a lukewarm initial review, arguing:

> The first half of the film works best, as Carpenter sets up an atmosphere of dread and unease that has always been his speciality. But the promise soon dissipates as the script becomes muddled and the film's Lovecraftian nightmares finally make themselves seen. (Salisbury, 1995)

To some it would seem that less *is* more, and it really is what you do not see that is most frightening. It could be argued, however, that Carpenter's rubber creations have a deliberately campy quality to them, perhaps an affectionate reference to the old science fiction B-movies (from 1953 perhaps?) that the director has so freely expressed this love and admiration for. His body of work is littered with references to vintage sci-fi pictures, the most obvious being Tommy and Lindsey watching *The Thing from Another World* in *Halloween*, which, of course, Carpenter would himself go on to remake. He employs a similar trick in *In the Mouth of Madness* when we see an old monster movie playing on the TV in Trent's motel room after he has escaped from Hobb's End. The film in question, *Robot Monster* (1953), a childhood favourite for Carpenter, is often regarded as one of the worst films ever made, thanks in part to its low production values and risible special effects. Still, for the fledgling filmmaker, such shortcomings did not prove a distraction, and with this small reference, not only is he paying his personal respects to an unloved B-movie, but also adding another layer of meta-intertextuality to his own film, drawing the lines between supposed fiction and understood fact. These films are just make-believe, but, as Trent has slowly come to understand by this point, real monsters do exist.

Elsewhere, *In the Mouth of Madness* showcases some extraordinary practical effects, created by KNB, the effects company founded by Robert Kurtzman, Greg Nicotero and Howard Berger. Mrs Pickman's monstrous transformation from kind old lady to axe-wielding octo-beast was actually shot in miniature, after the life-sized model failed to convince, resulting in a striking effect, the small scale lending an even more off-kilter edge to an already disturbing scene. Another highlight comes in the form of Styles' upside-down 'spider walk'. Reminiscent of the famously excised scene in *The Exorcist* in which Regan runs down the stairs backwards on all fours, this time with the added bonus of Styles' head being inverted too, it is one of the film's most genuinely perverse moments. This gag also recalls the body-twisting effects created by Screaming Mad George for the infamous 'shunt' scene at the climax of Brian Yuzna's *Society* (1989), a film which itself feels typically Lovecraftian in its depiction of monstrous evils existing just beneath the surface.

Styles' spider walk

Ultimately, in a film rife with nods and sly winks to the master of cosmic horror, it is that inescapable 'sense of cosmology and sense of otherness' deemed so vital by Del Toro, which makes In the Mouth of Madness so effective as a piece of Lovecraftian cinema. Right down to its fittingly downbeat ending, Carpenter's film is loaded with all of Lovecraft's favourite obsessions: the celestial immateriality of human existence, the futile concept of free will, the existence of other unknowable species and territories that threaten to impinge on our own, the access to forbidden knowledge that could result in the end of humanity. That crucial sense of otherness is all throughout In the Mouth of Madness, which may well be an original story, but feels like it is one that Lovecraft could have written himself, albeit with slightly more likeable characters.

So, perhaps Lovecraft is not so unfilmable after all? All it takes is a dash of empathy, a spot of humour, together with a sturdy grasp on his fatalistic philosophy – and cinematic gold is there for the taking ('gold' not being quite apt, perhaps, considering the film's less than dazzling box office performance). What truly makes In the Mouth of Madness so successful as a tribute to and extension of Lovecraft's writing, triumphantly elevating it above those frequently inferior adaptations which had come before, is the innate understanding that it is not the unspeakable monsters with their grotesque bodies and writhing tentacles which make his tales so terrifying. Instead, as we have come to understand is a common motif throughout Carpenter's cinema, it is the awful realisation that not only do we have no control of our own lives, but that humanity itself is little more than a cruel cosmic joke. The slimy beasts simply help drive the point home.

And speaking of cruel jokes, Carpenter makes the thoroughly un-Lovecraftian decision to end the film with a real zinger. As the final credits roll, some of the last words that appear on screen read:

> Animal interaction was monitored by the American Humane Association with on set supervision by the Toronto Humane Society. No animal was harmed in the making of this film. Human interaction was monitored by the Inter Planetary Psychiatric Association. The body count was high, the casualties are heavy.

Jokes might not have been Lovecraft's thing, but the sentiment here could not be more apt for the constant fatalist – human life is confirmed to be cheap. Of course, the body count was high, we are talking about the end of the world here. And what an end it is.

CHAPTER 4: 'YOU CAN FORGET ABOUT STEPHEN KING'

Whilst the works of H.P. Lovecraft are an unequivocal influence on *In the Mouth of Madness*, the literary associations do not end there. Cane's tales of terror are rooted firmly in Lovecraftian cosmicism, but there are also compelling links to the concerns of the gothic tradition's founding texts, and the meta-narrative complexities of postmodern literature.

But before we get to that, the figure of Sutter Cane himself, and his elevated celebrity persona, are very much a knowing homage to that other giant of horror fiction, Stephen King. Even the phonetics of King's name align him with the fictional writer (say both names out loud and hear the sonic resonance). In the real world, King is the most successful, and arguably the most influential writer of horror fiction there has ever been. In addition to his numerous published short stories, screenplays and works of nonfiction, King has written over 50 novels, including key works such as *Carrie*, *The Shining*, *The Stand*, *It* and *Misery*. His extraordinary output has seen him sell over 350 million books worldwide, positioning him as one of the biggest selling writers of all time. In the world of *In the Mouth of Madness*, none of this matters: Cane is king, as it were. As Styles so bluntly informs Trent, who appears oddly to have never heard of Cane (the first real indicator that Trent may not be the 'real' person that we/he believes he is), '*You can forget about Stephen King, Cane outsells them all*'. Cane has the vision of Lovecraft, coupled with the elevated popularity of King, making him the most influential writer on the planet – and as such, the most dangerous. In reality, the level of both King and Cane's successes are in stark contrast to those enjoyed by Lovecraft during his own lifetime. While he is now regarded as one of horror fiction's most influential and important writers, his work was not always held in such high regard. Unable to support himself financially from earnings for his work, Lovecraft died penniless at the age of 46 with most of his work out of print.

To best understand how Sutter Cane is as much a product of King as he is of Lovecraft, it is first worth noting the ways in which King himself is a graduate from the school of Lovecraft. King has always been vocal in his admiration for Lovecraft and, like Carpenter, has created work in tribute to his idol. King's short story 'Crouch End' is perhaps the most explicit. Originally published in the compendium *New Tales in the Cthulhu Mythos*, it concerns a couple attacked by a group of – yep, you guessed it – bizarre monsters, and even makes reference to one of Lovecraft's infamous deities, the mind-bendingly unfathomable Shub-Niggurath. Several of King's stories, including 'Gramma' (which appears in the *Skeleton Crew* collection), 'I Know What You Need' (from *Night Shift*) and his modern vampire novel *Salem's Lot*, are filled with Lovecraftian details and each make direct reference to the Necronomicon – like Lovecraft, King is also fascinated with the dangerous potential of the written word. King riffed on 'Colour Out of Space' with his story 'Weeds', which later served as the inspiration for the *Creepshow* (1982) segment, 'The Lonesome Death of Jordy Verrill', in which King himself played a backwoods (and backwards) farmer who undergoes a hideous botanical transformation following the crash landing of a meteor on his property. Meanwhile, his short story 'The Mist' boasts a legion of outer-dimensional monsters who cross over into our world with distinctly Lovecraftian consequences (something Frank Darabont took to the next level with his 2007 film adaptation, injecting an added level of nihilism beyond that found in King's text, supplying a bleak conclusion so hopeless it would make even H.P. himself depressed). Tributes to Lovecraft have continued in King's later work. Discussing his bracingly downbeat 2014 novel *Revival*, King stated, '*I wanted to use Lovecraft's Cthulhu mythos, but in a new fashion, if I could, stripping away Lovecraft's high-flown language*' (King in Elsworth, 2014). This quote succinctly highlights the stylistic differences between the two writers, King's arguably more traditional and accessible syntax is markedly different to Lovecraft's rather ostentatious vocabulary, even when striving for the same overall effect. It also recalls the manner in which *In the Mouth of Madness* translates Lovecraft's spirit onto the screen, softening his sharper edges to create something more accessible. Both King and Carpenter strive to maintain the core of Lovecraft's ideas, but present them in a more emotionally engaging (and commercially viable) way. Meanwhile, King and Lovecraft share another notable similarity; the creation of an entire fictional world for their characters to inhabit. King's equivalent of Lovecraft's Arkham is his imaginary Castle Rock, Maine, a sleepy New England town in which a disproportionate number of sinister and supernatural goings-on occur. And following in their footsteps, Sutter Cane is precisely this kind of world-maker, with his fantastical Hobb's End a sly mash up of Lovecraft and King's fictional stomping grounds.

One of the most frequently adapted authors in cinema, the majority of King's novels have made it to the screen in some shape or form, with more consistent success than those adaptations of Lovecraft's work. Some have argued that, like Lovecraft, there is something inherent to King's prose style (his frequent use of internal character dialogues and various literary tricks) that makes cinematic adaptations difficult. However, whether such notions are true or not, King's more conventional narrative arcs and empathetic characters make his writing fundamentally more adaptable than that of Lovecraft. The success (both critical and commercial) of such King adaptations as *Carrie* (1976), *The Shining* (1980), *The Dead Zone* (1983), *Misery* (1990), *The Shawshank Redemption* (1994) and *It* (2017) prove that, when handled effectively (perhaps with the same deft touch that De Luca brought to Lovecraft's writing?), King's prose can make for richly rewarding cinema.

In the Mouth of Madness was not the first time that Carpenter and Michael De Luca had turned to King for inspiration in their work, having both independently brought his stories to the screen on previous occasions. De Luca had written the screenplay for a short film adaptation of King's story 'The Lawnmower Man' in 1987 (not to be confused the with the 1992 film of the same name, which despite claims by the filmmakers, had nothing to do with King's original text), while Carpenter had directed an adaptation of King's killer car novel *Christine*, which dealt with similar themes of possession leading to the loss of free will that can be found throughout the director's *Apocalypse* Trilogy.

Similar to the ways in which it makes reference to Lovecraft both on a surface and on a deeper textual level, *In the Mouth of Madness* also positions King as far more than a nominal surrogate for Cane. In addition to allusions to King's celebrity and popularity, perhaps more significantly it incorporates many themes central to King's fiction into its own narrative. Placing an author as a central character is one of King's signature tropes, and like many of King's writer-protagonists, Cane acts as a conduit for the ensuing horror. And as in *In the Mouth of Madness*, the very process of writing in many of King's works – such as *The Shining*, *Misery*, *Bag of Bones*, *1408* – has the innate ability to either evoke, or ward off, some form of threat. In King's novel *The Dark Half*, the pseudonym of a bestselling author takes on a physical form after being 'killed off' by his creator. Typical of King's tendency for self-referentiality, the story was inspired by his relationship with his own pseudonym, Richard Bachman (to whom King 'dedicated' *The Dark Half*), the name under which he published such works as *The Running Man* and *Thinner* in an attempt to see if his work would sell without the power of his 'brand' behind it. In *The Dark Half*, like *In the Mouth of Madness*, the mere process of putting pen to paper is enough to bring forth a destructive, monstrous entity, with the author of said text being in the almost God-like position of creator, and ultimately, destroyer. Such meta-textuality can be found in King's *Dark Tower* series, in which he writes a fictional version of himself, also named Stephen King. Aspects of the author's real life (references to his existing works of fiction, his near fatal car accident from 1999) also appear within the series. Like Cane, the fictional King believes himself to be the writer of original stories, only to discover that he is merely a vessel used by a higher power. In this sense, perhaps neither Cane nor King are novelists at all, but merely diarists, or ghost writers, employed by an unknowable external force.

One might also think of King's short story 'Word Processor of the Gods' (featured in *Skeleton Crew*), in which a man discovers he can alter reality through the use of a magical typewriter. King's insistence that words have the (invariably destructive) ability to influence and shape the world around us is a key theme in Carpenter's film. Sutter Cane ultimately represents not just a fictionalised version of King the man, but in his ability to alter reality through his works of 'fiction', an extension of the fundamental concepts King has put forth in his written work.

If the spirits of Lovecraft and King clearly inhabit the fictional figure of Cane, then so too do the ghosts of earlier gothic literature, which often explored the concept of madness as a central theme within their texts. Be it a governess convinced of a spectral presence in Henry James' *The Turn of The Screw*, or a murderer's guilty mind making him imagine a heart beating below his floorboards in Edgar Allen Poe's 'The Tell-Tale Heart', madness in these stories is linked to an overactive imagination, to misreading the environments and misattributing sinister meaning to seemingly inexplicable events. And beyond the level of the text, madness was sometimes even part of the discourse (and mythos) around the creation and reception of these works. Pioneering gothic writer Ann Radcliffe, whose novel *The Mysteries of Udolpho* tells of a woman consumed by paranoid delusions of supernatural activity, is often claimed to have herself been driven mad by the content of her own horrific creations. Like the fictional Sutter Cane, Radcliffe spent her days in self-imposed isolation, creating the literary monsters that (supposedly) became real for her as she lost her mind. Susceptibility to the suggestion that horrors lurked beneath the benign surface of reality drove both the protagonist of Udolpho and her creator mad. This notion of susceptibility was indicative of a wider concern during the peak of gothic literature's popularity, that horror fiction was so potent it could literally drive the reader insane. Such concern was largely attributed to the female reader, and it is significant that in Carpenter's film, Styles – really the only substantial female character – is not just Cane's editor but an enthusiastic fan. When she hungrily reads Cane's manuscript, she is driven mad in precisely the way the Victorian establishment feared female readers would be by exposure to pulpy horror yarns. Trent, meanwhile, takes the position of disapproving male critic, and deems himself immune to the charms of such prose – and, to the danger it poses to the weak-of-mind. Thus the plot of *In the Mouth of Madness* links not only to the paranoid plots of gothic fiction, but also to the cultural fears attached to it; the myths of deranged authors, and in turn the susceptible consumer. If the writers themselves are not immune to the powers of their creations, then what chance does the regular reader have? As the solitary man we meet in the Hobb's End tavern puts it, '*reality is not what it used to be*'.

The hysteria concerning the supposed dangers of lurid gothic literature was surely part of its attraction for readers in the Victorian era – feelings still familiar to contemporary fans of horror books, films or games. Indeed, such dangers are often exploited as a key selling point; potential audiences are dared to confront perils of horror ('Dare you see *Saw*?'). *In the Mouth of Madness* engages directly with the supposedly corrupting capacity of the genre, and how attractive that is. At one point we see a bus advertising the imminent arrival of Cane's 'In the Mouth of Madness', with the tagline '*You'll go mad with fear…*'; but unlike the hyperbole commonly utilised by modern publishers and film studios, the danger in Carpenter's film is real, and thus we can only take this statement literally. Cane himself says of his latest publication, '*You must try reading my new one. The others have had quite an effect, but this one will drive you absolutely mad*'. His work is being sold on the very idea that it will irrevocably affect the minds of its readers. Obsession and insanity are merely advertising tricks. The mental health of the consumer is not there to be respected (or protected), it is there to be commodified and exploited.

Of course, in the case of Cane's work, readers would have been wise to take heed of Arkham's advertising campaign warnings, sidestepping the author's latest instead of

A bus advert for Cane's latest book

taking on the challenge, as once these beasts have been set free from their printed prison, they can no longer be stopped. In the original introduction to her seminal horror text *Frankenstein*, Mary Shelley stated, '*I bid my hideous progeny go forth and prosper*' (Shelley, 2003: 10). In much the same way that Cane unleashed his monsters upon humanity, so Shelley relinquished control over her heinous creation and set it loose into the world alone. Although she could not have known it at the time, with this quote she was in essence giving permission to the endless adaptations and various incarnations in which her monster has appeared over the years, not least in cinema. Shelley's sentiment deftly highlights the notion that once an artist has produced a work of art, it is no longer theirs, but the collective property of all those who invest in it. Shelley, like her very own Dr Frankenstein, or Sutter Cane, is the creator of life. A life which, once freed, cannot be controlled. The work itself becomes a monster, an avatar of the beast it describes.

As Cane's work spills out into the real world, the only way his ideas can successfully infiltrate the popular consciousness is for people to read them, or once the film version of 'In the Mouth of Madness' is released, to see them. As previously discussed, Cane's words are there to infect his readers. Language is a deadly virus spread from one reader to the next. Carpenter's former apocalyptic infections were spread physically (through alien infestation or satanic ooze), but here they are transmitted through storytelling. One can only be exposed to the disease if one chooses to read Cane's work, and thus the cumulative power of his prose is based solely on rates of consumption. In Bernard Rose's *Candyman*, in which a supernatural folk icon is summoned into the real world by a sceptical research student who is writing a thesis on urban legends, the titular villain recognises that his energy stems from the very act of being talked about, that without the sharing of his legend he would simply cease to exist. He explains: *'I am the writing on the wall, the whisper in the classroom. Without these things, I am nothing.'* For *Candyman*, or *Frankenstein*, or Sutter Cane, their horror can only continue to exist through the telling of their tales, like fairy stories passed down through generations. The very notion of evil is manifested into existence through a collective consciousness. In *The Cinema of John Carpenter*, Cane's work is described as *'vampire-like'* (Mulvey-Roberts in Conrich and Woods, 2004: 87), as it feasts on the lifeblood of its readers as a means of gaining momentum. Consumption is the key to prosperity, the reader is the vessel for spreading the fear. But while the tale at the heart of *Candyman* (a black slave murdered in the 1890s for impregnating a wealthy white woman) is rooted in folklore and spread through the old tradition of oral storytelling, Cane's tales are published works, supposedly new and available to purchase from your nearest bookstore. This disconnect between old and new, between ancient custom and modern commerce, is what sets these stories apart. In *Candyman* the story spreads organically; in *In the Mouth of Madness* it is there to be bought. Cane's readers are wilfully purchasing their own demise, adding another dimension to Carpenter's ongoing critique on the deadly perils of capitalist venture.

In the Mouth of Madness is influenced by a variety of literary sources, but Carpenter is also interested in exploring very the acts of reading and writing themselves. His is a film with distinct literary leanings, but Carpenter's medium is ultimately a visual one, and he employs various aesthetic techniques throughout to explore ideas around the tangibility (or intangibility) of the written word. Carpenter is invested in exploring the materiality of Cane's novels and the physical act of sifting through the pages of a book, both of which shape the visual language of the film and manifest in a variety of formal devices – or, should we say, flourishes, considering their bold originality. In one key scene, after Cane has told Trent to deliver his manuscript to Arcane, explaining how he cannot keep his monsters at bay for much longer, he proceeds to tear himself open, as though his image was printed on a sheet of paper. We can see that Cane's words appear on the other side of this rip in reality (a rip both literal and metaphorical), as though he is merely an illustration on the page of one of his own novels. As Trent approaches the

Cane tears himself open

tear and peers into the void beyond, Styles reads a passage from Cane's manuscript, 'In the Mouth of Madness'.

> Trent stood at the edge of the rift, stared into the illimitable gulf of the unknown, the Stygian world yawning blackly beyond. Trent's eyes refused to close. He did not shriek, but the hideous unholy abominations shrieked for him. As in the same second, he saw them, spill and tumble upward, out of an enormous carrion black pit, choked with the gleaming white bones of countless unhallowed centuries. He began to back away from the rift as the army of unspeakable figures, twilit by the glow from the bottomless pit, came pouring at him toward our world.

In this moment it becomes clear that Trent, and the events that have so far unfolded, are merely products of Cane's imagination. Trent is a character in Cane's new novel, a pawn in his literary game. It is extraordinary to witness Cane's image literally torn open. In De Luca's original script, the entire town of Hobb's End was going to get sucked into Cane's book at this point – but this had to be altered during production for budgetary reasons. The compromise made, that Cane tear himself open to reveal the gaping vastness of the 'Stygian world' behind him, is arguably a more interesting solution. It is almost as though the entire film has been processed on paper, rather than film stock. In spectacular fashion it alerts us, the viewer, to the fact that the story we have watched unfold is in fact an embedded narrative, written by the elusive Cane. And in doing so it plays with ideas about 'projection' and the supposedly vivid realities that we get absorbed in – on

Trent peers into the void

page, on screen – whose illusoriness we can forget. Much like Plato's cave dwellers, watching shadows on the wall, Carpenter's hybrid screen-page leads us to wonder about the substantiality of what we might take as reality. It is a flimsy reality that can be ripped open, as easily as tearing apart a piece of paper – or a screen. Like the printed pages of a novel, what we might take as reality may in fact be paper-thin.

This sequence also mirrors another moment in which Trent notices a rip in one of the posters for 'The Hobb's End Horror' which are plastered across the wall of a dark alley. Towards the end of the film he returns to the same location, this time fingering the tear, ripping it to reveal underneath the poster for Cane's next work, 'In the Mouth of Madness', on which his own likeness is portrayed. Once again, reality is rendered paper thin, a flimsy surface atop a deep void which can be easily torn open to reveal what

Another rip in reality

lies on the other side. In this case, it is Trent himself who appears beneath, a compelling indicator that he has crossed over, that he has left our reality. Or perhaps more accurately, that he never really belonged here in the first place. Trent's realisation that he is in fact a character in a fictional work ties in directly with Lovecraft's recurring themes of alternative dimensions, and profound doubts about the existence of free will – but meta-narrative structures and (justified) paranoia about other realities beyond and parallel to our own are not uniquely Lovecraftian. We might think of Philip K. Dick's early novel *Eye in the Sky*, which sees his characters travel through a series of alternate dimensions and subjective realities, or Muriel Spark's novel *The Comforters*, in which the main protagonist realises that she is the fictional creation in a novel, as does the titular character in Jostein Gaarder's philosophical exercise *Sophie's World*. The list could go on – in Paul Auster's *New York Trilogy* and Bret Easton Ellis' *Lunar Park*, both Auster and Ellis feature as characters within the story, much like King featured in the *Dark Tower* books, or Cane appears as a main protagonist in his latest work, blurring the lines between fantasy and reality, and further complicating the assumed role of the author as creator of a self-contained fictional world. This concept of multi-layered literary realities was drolly articulated in the original tagline for *In the Mouth of Madness*, which asked, '*Lived any good book lately?*'.

In his 1980 meta-textual novel *Land of Laughs*, American fantasy fiction novelist Jonathan Carroll apparently anticipates much of Carpenter's film with his story about a man who visits the fictional town created by his favourite novelist. Carroll's novel questions whether the town was the inspiration for the writer's work, or the work somehow created the town. Like Cane's Hobb's End, the novel plays a crafty game of 'which came first?'. The similarities between Carroll's book and Carpenter's film are acknowledged by the writer himself in an interview featured on his website. He states

> The screenwriter who wrote… *In the Mouth of Madness* happily told me that he stole most of the idea of my book for that film. But that only made me smile because I thought well, at least part of my idea gets to go up on a screen…. (Carroll, n.d.)

Carroll seems to agree with Arcane: a movie version is the endgame. Even the most popular books can only reach so far. Not everyone reads – but (nearly) everyone goes to the movies. The title of Carroll's book is significant too, conjuring up images of the

Trent's climactic laughter

final shot in Carpenter's film, in which a broken Trent descends into maniacal hysterics as he watches himself on screen. He too has entered the land of laughs, and it is clear this is a world from which he will never be able to return.

Mythological or mirage-like towns have also been explored several times on screen, most notably in Vincente Minnelli's musical *Brigadoon* (1954) in which two Americans stumble across a magical Scottish hamlet that only appears once every 100 years. Shlock gore-meister Herschell Gordon Lewis put his own grand-guignol spin on this wholesome tale a decade later with his film *Two Thousand Maniacs!* (1964), where the vengeful ghosts of the dead return every 100 years to claim the lives of centennial celebration revellers on a former Civil War site in an old-fashioned Deep South town. As with Trent and Styles in Carpenter's film, in both cases the characters within the films find themselves occupying spaces that should not exist, fantastical no man's lands, thus in turn throwing up questions of their own existence. Meanwhile the legacy of *In the Mouth of Madness* can be traced in *Silent Hill* (2006), a horror film based on a video game series which takes place in a fictitious ghost town. Unlike the temporary mythological spaces of Minnelli and Lewis' films, the town of Silent Hill is an otherworldly constant, a space that exists just outside of our reality, and thus bears a more direct relation to Hobb's End. However, fleeting or not, in each of these places the notion of artificial space is apparent. None of these fictional towns truly exist, much like the temporary unreality of a movie soundstage. The sceptical Trent himself makes direct reference to the concept of cinematic artifice, believing that the town of Hobb's

End is simply a constructed set, complete with '*special effects*' and '*hidden speakers*', with its residents nothing more than character actors. One might think of *The Truman Show* (1998), in which an unsuspecting man discovers his whole life to be a fabricated piece of reality TV, which subsequently lent its name to a psychotic delusion known as The Truman Show Delusion, or Truman Syndrome, whereby sufferers believe their entire lives to be elaborate works of fiction taking place on giant sound stages. By the climax of *In the Mouth of Madness*, Trent experiences the most acute case of Truman Syndrome imaginable, as he quite literally watches his life rendered as a work of fiction on the cinema screen.

'Milagro', an episode from the sixth season of *The X-Files*, also serves as an interesting counterpoint to the textual reflexivity of Trent's situation. In the episode, a writer working on a crime fiction novel predicts murders yet to occur and influences the course of events. Riffing on themes explored by King in 'Word Processor of the Gods', 'Milagro' presents a world in which the act of fiction writing shapes reality, blurring the distinctions of what is real and what is imagined. Both Cane and the literary antagonist of this episode are similar forces of evil, not only bringing forth the horrors that unfold, but robbing those around them of any control in the process. Mulder and Scully are rendered as works of fiction, denied the luxury of free will. They are special agents with no agency. The episode also marks a rare case in which the normally sceptical Agent Scully is the believer, while the devoutly believing Agent Mulder acts as dissenter, mirroring the relationship between Styles and Trent in which it is the female character who is open to paranormal possibilities, while the male character is hesitant to open himself up to the existence of alternate realities (although Trent's ultimate transformation from sceptic to believer does recall the ideological about turn experienced by Nada, the initially doubting anti-hero of Carpenter's *They Live*). And of course, *The X-Files*' iconic tagline 'Trust no one', could serve as a fitting sentiment for all the films in Carpenter's *Apocalypse* series.

Unlike René Descartes' well-known philosophical proposition, 'I think, therefore I am' (Descartes, 1637), in which he argues that the very notion of questioning one's own existence is indicative that one does in fact exist, the characters that inhabit John Carpenter's film are unable to think for themselves, and as such cease to be 'real' (real within the logic of the film, that is). This reminds us of *The Matrix* (1999), in which the protagonist, Neo, discovers the world he has lived in his whole life is not what it seems – that he has been tricked by evil machines that have created it. Once again, (as with *Scream*) we see how *In the Mouth of Madness* anticipates a major, supposedly cerebral, 1990s genre blockbuster – but once again, Carpenter's prototype presents a more complicated, more troubling version. In *The Matrix*, Neo can – and does – escape the fabricated reality of the 'matrix', and joins rebels in the 'real' reality. *In the Mouth of Madness* is less optimistic, and does not entertain the idea of escape to a more stable, authentic level of reality. *The Matrix* also maintains faith in Neo and his pals as individuals who can realise individual will and sense of authentic self. Not so in *In the Mouth of Madness*, where the malevolent choke hold on the individual is more intimate, and more fundamental. Carpenter's film imagines a world in which no human being has free will – they are not just in a fictional, insubstantial world, they are fictional in and of themselves. This existential conundrum makes for an interesting viewing experience, as we are asked to invest in characters whose legitimacy is constantly undermined. We are led to conclude that none of the characters in the film, the God-like Cane included, are 'real'. But, of course, they were never real, – we are watching a movie, and no movie character truly exists – a fact we are constantly reminded of. If much of mainstream narrative film draws the viewer in with the promise of characters one can identify with, and an immersion in make-believe, this Brechtian device of drawing attention to the constructedness of fiction (as a means of distancing the viewer) denies us these simple pleasures. But somehow Carpenter is no Brechtian spoilsport. Although a critique of capitalist venture is intrinsic to Carpenter's work, the 'fictionality' that he is drawing attention to here is not part of this political project – the aim of 'waking us up' to the constructedness of the world is not to draw our attention to injustice (to awaken us from Marxist 'false consciousness' as the Wachowski sisters are perhaps doing in *The Matrix*). Instead, he presents the pleasures – and horrors – of 'what-if?' mind games in the spirit of playful fun, as opposed to a rigorous critique of social realities.

The distancing techniques employed to disorientate the viewer (who might be expecting a more familiar horror ride), perhaps offer further reason as to why *In the Mouth of Madness* was initially something of a commercial disappointment. In much the same way that audiences of popular film are drawn to characters they can identify with, they also respond to concrete narratives and comprehensible conclusions. Carpenter's

The Thing proved challenging to viewers due to its fierce nihilism, but that seems nothing compared to this endeavour. By the conclusion of *In the Mouth of Madness* we can no longer trust Trent, nor can we trust Carpenter, and as a result, we can no longer trust ourselves.

CHAPTER 5: 'THE NEW BIBLE'

In its depiction of the all-knowing, omnipotent author, able to alter reality with the mere power of their words, *In the Mouth of Madness* elevates the figure of the writer to near-religious status. As Cane types away on his very own 'word processor of the Gods', he too becomes one of those Gods (or at the very least, a disciple of some description), with divine control over those in his literary kingdom. With this notion in mind, this chapter will explore the ways in which Carpenter's film repositions the writer from mere cultural commentator to modern day prophet, or untouchable celestial being, and how it utilises theological concepts to form the basis of its philosophical framework, ultimately presenting religious cultdom as an extension of Carpenter's critiques on mindless consumerism and his apocalyptic obsessions with the loss of individuality and free will.

In an interview published in Fangoria magazine shortly prior to the release of *In the Mouth of Madness*, Michael De Luca, in discussing his inspiration for the story, explained:

> I thought there was a way to take Lovecraft's most inspirational elements and weave them into a contemporary story. So I married his theme of ancient demigods waiting to get back into our world with the concept of an L. Ron Hubbard or a Stephen King, an author so immensely popular that his fans would actually follow his work with something like religious fanaticism. (De Luca in Rowe, 1994)

This quote does two interesting things. Firstly, it positions Hubbard, the founder of the controversial Church of Scientology, as foremost a writer of fiction as opposed to religious leader (something which will be picked up later in this chapter). Secondly, and more broadly speaking, it alludes to the wider concept of religion as a recurring thematic device in horror cinema, and the near spiritual fervour with which works of fiction can be embraced by their most ardent devotees.

Catholicism, with its supposed stability and widely understood internal logic, has undoubtedly proven to be the horror genre's most repeated source of religious inspiration in terms of overall themes, narratives and iconography. *The Exorcist* franchise, *Rosemary's Baby* (1968), *Stigmata* (1999) and John Carpenter's very own *Prince of Darkness* are just a few horror films to explore the relationship between the Catholic religion and sinister events. Another famous example, *The Omen* (1976) imagined the arrival of the Devil on Earth in the form of a young boy named Damien, who would grow up to be a US ambassador in *The Omen III: The Final Conflict* (1981). Not only was the adult incarnation of Damien played by Sam Neill, but in the first film David Warner (Dr Wrenn in *In the Mouth of Madness*) played a prominent role, which lends an amusing dimension to the opening scenes of Carpenter's film in which a sceptical Warner visits Neill, who is covered in crucifixes and babbling on about the apocalypse. Such 'religious horror' films seek to exploit familiar Catholic imagery, albeit with an added sense of mischief. However, in terms of intellectual engagement, they often do little more than recycle the traditionally accepted Catholic notions of good and evil (God as good, the Devil as evil, just to be clear), thus presenting a (fairly simplistic) conservative worldview which ultimately confirms the good/evil binary it often attempts to play with.

While by no means a straightforward morality tale, Carpenter's film does still in some regards play into this familiar vision; Cane is the bad guy (Devil?), Trent the (flawed) good guy out to stop him. It is perhaps only natural that theological leanings manifest via Christian idioms in an American film, so inherent is the religion throughout many aspects of American culture. In one scene, Trent watches a TV news report detailing the Sutter Cane craze in which the newscaster speculates as to whether Cane is, '*A harmless pop phenomenon, or deadly prophet of the printed page*'. Like the Book of Revelation, the 'prophet' Cane's manuscript foretells the apocalypse, positioning him not just as a mere writer of fiction, but seer of things to come and mouthpiece for a higher source. The trope of an antagonist as divine being or religious vessel is not uncommon within horror; in the *Hellraiser* film series (which presents physical pain as a gateway to a state of almost transcendental religious ecstasy), Pinhead, the lead figure of a group of sadomasochistic extradimensional beings called the cenobites, positions himself as a modern day God (or anti-God) through specific reference to the holy sacrament, exclaiming, '*This is my body. This is my blood. Happy are they who come to my supper*', in *Hellraiser III: Hell on Earth* (1992). On another occasion, when a character, taken aback by the appearance of this alien body, exclaims, '*Jesus Christ*', Pinhead drolly replies, '*Not quite*'. Similarly, in Wes Craven's original *A Nightmare on Elm Street*, shortly before killing Tina, Krueger mischievously informs her, '*This is God*'. Like Pinhead or Krueger, Cane believes his own hype, proudly positioning himself as some kind of religious deity. In the scene with Trent and Cane in the confessional, Cane refers to his latest book as the '*new Bible*', before going on to inform Trent that, '*More people believe in my work than believe in the Bible*'. His disciples are his readers, impatiently waiting for the latest verse in the Gospel according to Cane. In a world where the writer is a God, and fiction is both his means of communication and source of power, the horror novel is elevated to the level of scripture. It becomes a truly potent text, with awesome destructive powers.

In that same news report, the newsreader also questions, '*When does fiction become religion, and are his fans dangerous?*'. And by fans, we are talking rabid consumers. This is familiar Carpenter territory: wariness of the power of consumer culture to generate mindless zombies. The news anchor's statement also calls to mind real-life instances of literary hysteria, like fans of the hugely popular *Harry Potter* or *Twilight* sagas queuing overnight to access the latest instalments of their favourite books on the morning of release. These impatient fans are much like Cane's followers, perhaps guilty of an almost evangelical monomania, rather than an informed, critical appreciation of the texts themselves. Their devotion recalls the scenes of frenzy at the book stores selling Cane's newest publications. Such devotion to literary pop phenomena ultimately affords the author an almost quasi-religious power (with the occasional spot of fan rioting proving an unfortunate side-effect). Of course, when it comes to Cane, who is *actually* in possession of omnipotent power via the word, the frenzy is justified (and so, critique of consumerism is not really the chief issue here, as in, for example, *They Live*).

The newsreader's concerns as to the power of Cane's prose calls to mind the first verse of the St John's Gospel: '*In the beginning was the Word, and the Word was with God, and the Word was God*', and the subsequent line, '*The Word became flesh and made his dwelling among us*'. Similar to John's scripture, Cane's words are themselves reified – they are no longer intangibly linguistic, but become realised on a physical plane. As in *Candyman*, the power of the word and the sharing of stories is understood as paramount to the creation of new life, and the construction of belief, myth and legend. Cane explains that '*Religion seeks discipline through fear, yet doesn't understand the true nature of creation.*' By this, he implies that a true, powerful faith involves the interaction of a god/writer, his word, and his believer/reader – a kind of collaboration which has the power to create a reality. Cane continues to say that, before now, '*No one's ever believed it enough to make it real. The same cannot be said of my world.'* In the world of *In the Mouth of Madness*, the constructedness of religion and reality is drawn attention to; but, crucially, it is the reader, not the author, who is needed to make the imaginative world of the author real. Ultimately, it is Cane's acolytes in Hobb's End, and his readers in the 'real' world, who make his word flesh.

Everything that occurs within the narrative of *In the Mouth of Madness* is a result of the words which pour off of Cane's prophetic pen. Cane writes it, and, through the collective power of his readers, so it becomes. But while Cane is controlling this fictional universe, it is John Carpenter who in turn controls him. In filmmaking terms, the director is deemed God, the omnipotent dictator of all that will occur. His actors, much like the characters in Cane's work, have their actions prescribed to them. They have a script and are given directions, rendering them as little more than puppets with no free will. Alfred Hitchcock allegedly once referred to actors as 'animated props', articulating (perhaps cruelly) the sense of autonomy he felt as the master of ceremonies, positioning the director as the wizard behind the curtain, controlling events from behind the scenes. It could perhaps be argued that horror directors, more than any other directors specialising within specific genre boundaries, exert a level of control over their viewers which is quite unique. The manner in which horror filmmakers control the emotions of viewers through means of fear and anxiety is in itself a form of emotional domination, with the term 'master of horror' often used to describe the most celebrated genre auteurs (Carpenter himself contributed two episodes to the TV series known by that very name). By the end of *In the Mouth of Madness*, if we are in any doubt as to who is pulling the strings, Carpenter positions his film itself as the ultimate text. Books will only get you so far, film will finish the job. With Cane little more than a pawn in the director's game, the film we are watching is ultimately the Gospel according to John Carpenter.

Of course, Carpenter's Gospel is rife with other references to Christian beliefs and iconographies. Cane's name itself is not just a nod to Stephen King, but also to Cain from the Bible, perpetrator of the first murder, that of his brother Abel. With this single act of fratricide, Cain was cursed and banished from his home. Just as Cain was the first murderer, Cane would essentially be the last, exterminating all of humanity with his literary weapon. Also, the name of Hobb's End goes beyond the Nigel Kneale reference, to take on theological significance. Hob was in fact a medieval term for the Devil, also known as 'old hob'. Coupled with the use of 'end', the name of the town takes on an ominous eschatological significance, quite literally translating as the devil's apocalypse – a rather apt place for Carpenter's end of the world trilogy to conclude. One might also think of philosopher Thomas Hobbes, the archetypal Enlightenment thinker who championed the idea of the rational individual. Hobb's End (or should that be Hobbe's End?) might then also refer to the death of this rational individual that is so central to Enlightenment thinking.

The religious implications and concerns of *In the Mouth of Madness* are not only found within its wider theoretical and narrative frameworks, or in fleeting nominal references. One of the film's most important locations provides a fittingly hallowed backdrop to the unfolding holy horrors. While Cane's Hobb's End may appear on the surface like any other sleepy New England hamlet, the imposing Byzantine church at the town's centre, which offers sanctuary to the reclusive writer, is in stark contrast to the unassuming simplicity of the otherwise quaint village architecture. The building itself is an existing structure located just north of Toronto in Markham (a name deliciously close to Lovecraft's own Arkham), Ontario, known as The Cathedral of Transfiguration. Closed as a place of worship in 2006, this former Slovak Greek Catholic cathedral provided the perfect location for Cane's Black Church, with its striking mosaics, grandiose marble walls and distinctive bulbous domes making it feel both impressive and defiantly out of place. The inside of the church, however, was shot on a sound stage, allowing for the required visual trickery to create a sense of otherworldly unease.

Trent and Styles approach the Black Church

Within the imposing walls of the Black Church, and outside of them too, the image of the crucifix is a recurring visual theme. Early on in the film, Trent covers himself in crudely drawn crosses as a means of protecting himself from the encroaching evils he fears are closing in on him. In a later scene in the Church, Trent awakens in a confessional, with Cane on the other side. Trapped in the position of subordinate, with Cane acting as the High Priest, light spills into Trent's booth from the outside, decorating his face in a grid-like shadow pattern. This striking effect is reminiscent of the crucifixes he will later adorn his skin with, acting as an ominous portent of things to come (or indeed a flashback to what the viewer has already seen).

Shadows across Trent's face

Writing on Trent's face

Elsewhere in the church, a large black inverted cross is visible on one of the walls. The symbol of the inverted cross derives from the story of St Peter, who was crucified upside-down out of his own respect for Jesus. In light of this, the inverted cross is often used in Catholic faith as a symbol of humility in comparison with Jesus. However, in more recent times the inverted cross has been adopted as an anti-Christian, blasphemous symbol with associations with Satanism and occult activity. In this respect, the inverted crucifix signals the evil contained within Cane's church, and its position as an alternative, ungodly place of worship.

Christianity, and the recognisable icons associated with it, may represent the most common framework for religion in Western horror cinema, although there are numerous films which explore alternative belief systems. *The Wicker Man* (1973) takes its inspiration from Celtic Paganism, while the Sam Raimi-produced *The Possession* (2012), about a possessed dybbuk box had its roots very firmly is Judaism. *The Sacrament* (2013) riffs on the concept of religious cultdom, focusing on the demise of a Jonestown-like religious sect, and Wes Craven's *The Serpent and the Rainbow* (1988) presents a fantastical take on voodoo. Whilst the specific religions they focus on may be different, most of these films ultimately still boil down to a fairly straightforward take on the traditional notions of good versus evil as seen in those Catholic horrors previously mentioned. This is markedly different to the Scientological angle that De Luca's earlier quote hinted at, which has more unsettling implications, as indicated by Hubbard's dual role as author and religious leader, as sci-fi novelist and messianic force in the real world.

Although Scientology displays a tendency towards the fantastical as well as an investment in the existence of alternative worlds and realities, *In the Mouth of Madness*, through the dualities and similarities shared by Hubbard and Cane, might be the only time that the controversial religion has provided the basis for a horror film (although the shocking claims of human rights infringements put forth in Alex Gibney's documentary *Going Clear: Scientology and the Prison of Belief* (2015) were certainly frightening). For those uninformed, Scientology is a belief system developed by L. Ron Hubbard, the seeds of which emerged in his book *Dianetics*, published in 1950. The basis for Hubbard's theory is that all humans are immortal beings, trapped on Earth for millions of years having been banished from their home planet. These beings are referred to by Hubbard as 'thetans', and all thetans have multiple past lives, both on this Earth and beyond it. Central to the religion is a process known as 'auditing', in which, through a lengthy (and not financially inexpensive) process of analysis, lost thetans are able to liberate themselves from their human forms and reclaim their true selves. Essentially Scientology is about understanding one's own spiritual self through the acceptance of three central concepts: that we are immortal, that our lives extend beyond this current one, and that our capabilities are unlimited, although not currently realised. Scientology thus depends on the sanctity of an authentic and unique self, that the Church can help us access. This is, of course, at odds with Carpenter's trilogy which depicts the eventual breakdown of free will and individuality. As discussed, Carpenter is with Lovecraft, both gloomily undermining human exceptionalism. For Lovecraft, we are not secretly magical thetans, but insignificant beings at the mercy of an intergalactic order of Gods.

While there may be inherent differences between the individualist beliefs of Scientology and Carpenter's more nihilistic Lovecraftian point of view, there are many compelling crossovers which align the controversial religion with the cosmic terrors of *In the Mouth of Madness*. Like Lovecraft (or even Cane), Hubbard started out as a writer of science fiction. As a religious leader it could be argued he has continued to behave as such. His construction of a new faith is not dissimilar to the world-building that an author undertakes, and through his followers he has welcomed millions into this Hubbardian universe. Scientology's doctrine is underpinned by the sense of an alternative reality and waking us up to what's 'really going on', but the irony is that Hubbard has used fiction as the basis on which to build a new artifice, the transparency of which is absurd, but also powerful. Authors can wield the power to generate a kind of reality that goes beyond the imaginative, and it is that ability which connects Hubbard and Cane. When we laugh at Scientology, are we like the enlightened Trent laughing at the cinema screen?

Hubbard's early short stories were often printed in the same publications that also ran Lovecraft's tales. Although the pair display a fundamental difference in their position on humankind's agency (or lack thereof) in the world, the two do share many significant similarities. Both writers of science fiction tales, each of them used their fictional stories to explore the concept of other worlds existing beyond our own. Both men wrote of vast galactic systems and inhabited universes, and documented how aliens first came to Earth tens of millions of years ago, only for any evidence of such civilisations to have been long since buried. As Lovecraft did in his story 'The Whisper in Darkness', both writers also explored the untapped resources of the mind, in its ability to travel billions of years and miles through space.

In his essay, 'Cthulu vs Xenu', which explores the similarities between the two writers, Jason Colavito explains how the pair were producing works of fiction around the same time, leading to striking parallels. Colavito says:

> It would go far beyond the evidence to suggest Hubbard borrowed his cosmology from Lovecraft, but the core concepts of ancient aliens, buried civilisations, and mental transfer across time are all ideas that Lovecraft wrote about in stories that Hubbard almost certainly would have read. (Colavito, 2011)

Of course, Lovecraft didn't go on to create a religion.

Given that Sutter Cane is in part a product of Lovecraft, such similarities in their work makes a compelling case that Cane is also of Hubbardian descent: a cultural icon bringing forth news on alien lifeforms and alternate intergalactic realities. Both Hubbard and Cane are writers of fiction whose work has, through one means or another, taken on 'real' significance for their readers. They are the inventors of new religions, prophets informed from a higher, extra-terrestrial being. It is perhaps not a coincidence either that, in much the same way that Cane's work is claimed to influence the minds of his less stable readers, Scientology has come under frequent criticism for allegedly brainwashing or performing a kind of mind control on its followers. Such high-profile followers of the religion as John Travolta or Tom Cruise have publicly denied any such claims, although in a curious case of synchronicity, it is worth noting that Cruise was at one point attached to Guillermo Del Toro's high-profile but doomed attempt to bring Lovecraft's 'At the Mountains of Madness' to the screen.

Among Hubbard's many novels was *Typewriter in the Sky*, the tale of a man who finds himself transposed within the narrative of his friend's book. While its title was a likely source of inspiration for Stephen King's aforementioned 'Word Processor of the Gods', Hubbard's meta vision of a man existing within the fictional pages of someone else's written work preempts the conceptual essence of *In the Mouth of Madness*. In addition to this, one of Hubbard's earlier unpublished manuscripts, 'Excalibur', which laid many of the foundations which would go on to form Scientology, was claimed by the author to be so dangerous that those who read it went insane and were driven to suicide. Not only was Hubbard the creator of self-reflexive works in which his protagonists were characters in works of fiction, but his other stories were allegedly so potent that, much like early Gothic literature, they could make their readers go out of their minds. As with the crossover between Hubbard and Lovecraft, the similarities between the Scientology founder and the fictional Cane are equally striking.

While most horror films that dabble in themes of religion boil down to a rather conservative battle between good and evil, *In the Mouth of Madness* ultimately offers up something far more provocative than the familiar morality tale. Traditionally understood notions of good and evil are very much part of the fabric of the film (this is a horror movie after all), but through a critique of Scientological constructs as seen in the mirroring of Cane with Hubbard, the primary conflict could be more accurately viewed as an internal, existential one. Unlike Judeo-Christian faith, Scientology is not invested in the idea of one omnipotent God (or malevolent Devil), focusing instead on the individual's search for true understanding and transcendence beyond an illusory earthly, human reality (perhaps making it more similar to Eastern faith, like Buddhism). As such, the religio-horror of *In the Mouth of Madness* presents an interesting contrast to the over-familiar Catholic terrors we are used to seeing on screen; inspired by Scientology, Carpenter's film not only relishes the depiction of a crazed Hubbardian novelist-messiah, but the very intrigue and horror at its core stems from uncertainty about the nature of our Earthly reality, and the idea that an absurd fictional construct may be just as valid.

CHAPTER 6: 'ISN'T HE THE GUY THAT WRITES THAT HORROR CRAP?'

In the Mouth of Madness is many things. It is a tribute to H.P. Lovecraft and an homage to Stephen King. It is a critique of religious fanaticism, and a comment on the fragility of human existence. But, perhaps more than anything, *In the Mouth of Madness* is a film about horror. A loving tribute to one of cinema's most consistently misunderstood and vilified modes of artistic expression, the film scrutinises and questions the very nature of fear and how it affects its audience, demanding the genre be both celebrated and given the respect it deserves. In doing so, it positions John Carpenter himself at the very centre, self-reflexively pondering his role as artist and creator of horrific images.

In its rigorous dissection of the genre, *In the Mouth of Madness* offers an interesting companion piece to *Wes Craven's New Nightmare*, which took a similarly postmodern view of horror cinema and its position within wider culture. In his film, Wes Craven depicts a world in which Freddy Krueger and the *Nightmare on Elm Street* franchise are an existing part of the 'real world' popular consciousness. Several actors and production crew from the series play fictionalised versions of themselves, including Heather Langenkamp (final girl Nancy from the first film) and Craven himself. In this meta-mindbender, the development of a new Freddy film has allowed Krueger to break free of his celluloid prison and cross over into 'reality'. Now Langenkamp must assume the fictional role of Nancy in an attempt to destroy Freddy once and for all. Craven and Carpenter's films share many obvious similarities: a supposedly fictional evil crossing over into the 'real world', a constant discussion of the role of horror fiction as a potent cultural force, and the role of the filmmaker (or writer) as an omnipotent creator of strange new worlds. This last point is addressed in *New Nightmare* during a scene in which Craven, playing Craven, discusses his script for a new *Nightmare* movie with Langenkamp. Explaining how his ideas come at night, Craven says, '*I wish I could tell you where this script is going. I don't know. Look, I dream a scene, I write it down the next morning. Your guess is as good as mine as to how it ends.*' With this observation, the fictional 'Craven', like Sutter Cane (or indeed Stephen King in the *Dark Tower* series), becomes a conduit for the evils of another reality. Through the process of writing them down, they become real (In the beginning was the word… and the word was made flesh). Similarly, in *In the Mouth of Madness*, Cane admits at one point, *'For years, I thought I was making all this up. But they were telling me what to write… giving me the power to make it all real. And now it is.'* Both 'Craven' and Cane appear to be in control, but in truth are as powerless as those who inhabit their works. They are vessels for a higher power, simply using the mediums of literature and film as a means of spreading the word. The ones truly in control are Craven (as director) and Carpenter. The film could well serve as Carpenter's response to Craven's film, and extension of its ideas. 'John Carpenter's New Nightmare', if you will.

Craven and Carpenter's films each place the writing process itself as central to their narratives, both in the ways in which fictional characters dictate how the story will unfold, and also the postmodern techniques of highlighting the written fabrication of reality to the viewer. Throughout *In the Mouth of Madness* characters make continual reference to the notion of being 'written'. In a twist on Descartes' aforementioned quote, *'I think, therefore I am'*, Sutter Cane tells Trent, *'You are what I write'*, which could be translated as *'I write, therefore you are'*. Elsewhere, in a scene between Styles and Trent, she explains, *'Cane's writing me. He wants me to kiss you… Because it's good for the book'*. This line cleverly justifies any moments that might be considered implausible, or any character actions that seem out of place. In the world of fiction, anything is possible, and all bets are off. This in particular explains the moments of, somewhat forced, sexual tension between Trent and Styles. While the two display a passable chemistry, their more flirtatious moments, or scenes in which they actually kiss seem oddly out of place. This is not only an amusing comment on the need for a romantic interest in cinema, whether or not it actually serves the plot in question, but also reflects Lovecraft's tendency to stray away from romantic storylines and his difficulty in drawing out fully rounded human characters.

A recognition of having been 'written' is again apparent in the scene in the bar when Trent tries to dissuade one of the Hobb's End residents from killing himself. Seemingly resigned to his destiny, the man explains, *'I have to. He wrote me this way'*, before blowing his brains out. It is worth noting the man in question is played by Wilhelm von Homburg who also portrayed Vigo the Carpathian in *Ghostbusters II* (1989), the demonic subject of the film's central painting. Like the character in Carpenter's film, Vigo is immortalised (or trapped) in a work of art, destined to live out his creator's macabre intentions. Just as the man in the bar professes that he is powerless to fight his character, Vigo might also have said, '*I have to. He painted me this way*'.

John Carpenter himself, when discussing the film, pays deferential reverence to the original source text. Referring to his rigid adherence to De Luca's script, he explained, sounding like one of the characters in the movie. '*You have to be true to the material. It was written that way*' (Carpenter in Boulenger, 2003: 233). Both on-screen and off the written word has absolute power. It was written and so it shall be. Echoes of *Wes Craven's New Nightmare* become apparent once again, particularly in regards to the fictional script within that film. At the conclusion, Heather Langenkamp (like Styles does in Carpenter's film) reads aloud from typed pages, the events she describes being mirrored in the real-life actions of the characters. Once again, the script dictates the action, and those characters who inhabit this universe are merely players, forced to live out what is printed on the page, just as the actors themselves do as they recite their lines of dialogue.

Like Carpenter's film, *Wes Craven's New Nightmare* failed to cause much impact at the box office, proving the lowest grossing entry in the original series, taking less than half of the highest grosser, *A Nightmare on Elm Street 4: The Dream Master* (1988). But while *New Nightmare* went somewhat under the radar on initial release in 1994, Craven hit it big a couple of years later when *Scream* kick-started the postmodern horror craze of the late 1990s. Unlike the cerebral complexities of *New Nightmare*, or *In the Mouth of Madness*, *Scream* was a far more straightforward realisation of a self-reflexive horror universe. Although the characters in *Scream* make frequent reference to other films, the film itself mostly functions as a fairly conventional slasher. Both Carpenter and Craven's earlier films paved the way for the self-reflexivity of *Scream*, leading to a resurgence in the genre, and making horror once again hip and relevant. While it takes a certain level of audience engagement and commitment to unearth the deeper layers of meaning and hidden complexities of both *New Nightmare* and *In the Mouth of Madness* (be that in an understanding of existentialist philosophies or Lovecraftian theory, for example), *Scream* offered a far more direct and accessible shot of meta-pleasures, and a far more palatable (less nihilistic, more playful) celebration of the horror genre.

Scream's success led to a glut of self-aware slashers, including *I Know What You Did Last Summer* (1997) (also penned by *Scream* scribe Kevin Williamson), *Urban Legend* (1998) and *Cherry Falls* (2000). While the classic horror formula of diminishing returns eventually kicked in, one of its more interesting descendants, and one unarguably indebted to *In the Mouth of Madness*, is *The Cabin in the Woods* (2012). What begins as a seemingly straightforward *Evil Dead* knock-off morphs into a sardonic postmodern exercise in which the central characters come under attack by a vast array of familiar creatures from the pantheon of horror history. Teasingly Lovecraftian in its central concept of alternate realities that house macabre beasts, *The Cabin in the Woods* proved the continued influence of Carpenter's film on contemporary horror cinema. But while the likes of *Scream* and *The Cabin in the Woods* dealt liberally in humour, Carpenter's film is much more serious in its approach. That is not to say his signature wry humour is not present, in fact there are jokes littered throughout, not only in Trent's sardonic wit, but also in much of the dialogue which walks a fine line between bracingly heartfelt and knowingly corny. But while the film may well be a fun ride, the horror at its heart is not ironic, it is deadly serious.

The genre self-reflexivity of *In the Mouth of Madness* is evident from the very first frames. As the pages of Cane's 'The Hobb's End Horror' roll off the whirring printing presses, an advert for his next book appears on the back cover. The text reads '*In the Mouth of Madness, coming soon*'. In fact, the film has already begun. Carpenter is letting us know that there is no time to waste, so sit back and prepare yourself for the onslaught of madness. Also visible on the book's jacket is its tagline, '*If this book doesn't scare you to death, you're already dead*', a nod to the tagline for *Phantasm* (1979) – '*If this one doesn't scare you, you're already dead!*' – which itself had a tinge of cosmic horror in its tale of an otherworldly undertaker and his legion of diminutive zombies. From the outset, Carpenter is acknowledging the existence of other horror films, and positions his own work within that well-populated world.

Such intertextual playfulness continues into the opening act, in which Trent is committed to the asylum. Almost a caricature of the figure of the madman, Trent is seen bound in a straightjacket, screaming of his sanity. Filming as though through a gothic filter, Carpenter bathes the sequence in a dark hue, illuminated with sporadic flashes of bright lightning. Trent says to his doctor, '*You're waiting to hear about my "them", aren't you? Every paranoid* schizophrenic has one.' Trent's cognisance of the constructed performance of insanity, coupled with the over-the-top horror stylings of the scene, and the knowing humour of Sam Neill's delivery, make the whole sequence feel distinctly unreal. We are clearly in horror movie territory here. One could almost imagine being in Dr Frankenstein's laboratory, or sharing a cell with the unhinged Renfield from *Dracula*. From the start Carpenter is clear that the unfolding film will be an exercise in genre – what it means, what it looks like, and what it does to us. With this self-awareness also comes further telling references to previous genre classics, most notably in the form of Saperstein, the doctor that Trent is speaking to, who shares his name with the corrupt doctor in *Rosemary's Baby*, an early indicator that we are not to trust anyone (not even doctors) in this dystopian world of terror.

As he continues to profess his sanity, a chorus of other inmates kicks in, each claiming to also be of sound mind. The droll humour of the sequence escalates until, in an attempt to sooth the riled up inmates, 'We've Only Just Begun' by easy-listening stalwarts The Carpenters pours out of the building's loudspeakers, to which Trent promptly cries, '*Oh no, not The Carpenters!*'. Far more than a cheeky dig at MOR music, this moment, like the earlier announcement that 'In the Mouth of Madness' is coming soon, now lets us know that the horrors have officially begun. But 'only just', there is plenty more in store, so don't get comfortable yet. The fact that it is The Carpenters who deliver this announcement also provides the film with one of its best gags, giving Trent, or rather Sam Neill, the chance to express his director's name with obvious disdain. It is our first clear sign that Carpenter is in control here, with Trent left powerless to his every whim. Carpenter has only just begun with him, and with us.

While foremost an exercise in horror and a deconstruction of the genre, Carpenter's film riffs on other cinematic styles throughout, further contributing to the overall sense of self-reflexivity and cine-literacy. The quarrelsome banter between Trent and Styles betrays Carpenter's love for screwball comedies, particularly *His Girl Friday* (1940) and the comedic works of Howard Hawks, something also evident in many of his other films, most notably the fast-paced whimsy of *Big Trouble in Little China*. Elsewhere, in an early scene in which Trent is seen exposing a man for insurance fraud, Carpenter plays it as a hard-boiled detective piece, right down to the moody music and smoky interiors of his *mise-en-scène*. The fact that Trent is a respected insurance fraud investigator is significant.

He makes a living uncovering the truth and exposing the lies. How ironic that he should himself ultimately prove to be a work of fiction in the end, part of a fabrication that he was unable to spot. Far more than mere inconsequential nods to some of Carpenter's favourite films, such moments of self-awareness further add to the unreality of the film, disrupting the viewer's immersion within the text, highlighting the constructedness of the cinematic world as fictional space by trading in recognisable and consistent generic conventions.

Trent in hard-boiled detective mode

Carpenter's sense of humour and playful irreverence is an essential part of the film's overall texture, yet in spite of this *In the Mouth of Madness* is no joke. This is the work of a director demanding to be taken seriously. Perhaps more than any other form of narrative cinema, the horror genre is the most consistently vilified and most readily dismissed. Carpenter himself has often reflected on the lack of respect afforded filmmakers working in the genre, once exclaiming:

> Horror directors are just a little bit more respectable than pornographers. Just a little bit! I've never really had much respectability as a director, certainly not like some of my peers. (Carpenter in Conrich and Woods, 2004: 178)

Although this quote sees Carpenter seemingly resigned to a life of being artistically undervalued (as has happened to him throughout his career), *In the Mouth of Madness* hints at a genuine frustration toward the situation, with the film functioning as a misunderstood filmmaker's attempt to validate the cultural worth and societal significance of a maligned genre. Trent himself represents the voice of the cynics, those who regard horror as throwaway, unsophisticated trash. The fact that Trent has seemingly never heard of Cane when he is first brought in to head up the manhunt shows a wilful lack of engagement with horror fiction in popular culture, despite Cane being a worldwide cultural icon. It seems impossible that Trent would have next to no idea who Cane was, and in denying knowledge of him, Trent seemingly indicates that Cane is simply not worthy of his attention, even on the most peripheral level. Trent goes on to describe Cane as a *'cash cow'*, as though literature of this kind could hold no artistic value or cultural significance; it is merely a money spinner, sold to philistines with no concept of high art. Even more blatantly, Trent disregards Cane's entire body of work, labelling it simply *'horror crap'*, and thus dismissing an entire genre outright.

Styles, on the other hand, is the voice of those horror fans (and more enlightened critics and academics) who treat the genre with due reverence, those who recognise its invaluable impact on culture and its innate ability to reflect the horrors of society back from the screen like a macabre mirror. In her book on the genre, Brigid Cherry reflects on how horror cinema is *'flexible and adaptable in its encompassing of the cultural moment, giving scope for filmmakers to encode changing socio-cultural concerns with ease'* (Cherry, 2009: 11). She goes on to argue that, *'since fear is central to horror cinema, issues such as social upheaval, anxieties about manmade and natural disasters, conflicts and wars, crime and violence, can all contribute to the genre's continuation'* (ibid.). While Cherry argues for the power of horror as a tool for political and/or social commentary, others note the genre's ability to convey the broader implications of existential anxieties and the ways in which the genre tackles complex philosophical ideas around existence. Writing about Lovecraft's cosmic horror in his book *The Philosophy Of Horror*, Noël Carroll explains how, *'The attraction of supernatural horror is that it provokes a sense of awe which confirms a deep-seated human conviction about the world, viz., that it contains vast unknown forces'* (Carroll, 2000: 162). Reacting to Trent's dismissal, Styles argues that perhaps Cane's work is simply *'too sophisticated'* for him, implying that its hidden depths can only be understood and appreciated by a more inquisitive mind. With this off-hand remark, the film makes the bold claim that it is not the horror genre that is dumb, but those who fail to understand its significance. If we are to accept the theory that we are watching the film version of Cane's book, and that all dialogue therein is his ('Sutter Cane's *New Nightmare*'), then such moments in which Styles celebrates the brilliance and complexities of Cane's work are amusingly self-congratulatory. The film is a chance for Carpenter to argue a case for the importance of horror and to give himself a well-deserved pat on the back. Through the figure of Trent he can have his revenge on those who doubted the power of horror, whilst by living vicariously through the figure of Cane, Carpenter can assert his position as the ultimate auteur.

Trent backtracks somewhat once he has read some of Cane's work. Immersed in the depraved pages of his novels, Trent admits, '*The funny thing is that they're kind of better written than you'd expect. They sort of get to you in a way. I don't know if it's his style of writing or his use of description or whatever, but…*'. High praise indeed from one so defiantly dismissive just moments earlier. Such surprise as to the power that horror can hold is endemic to a genre so frequently undervalued. Cane's counterpart Stephen King, for example, is often (derisively) labelled a mere horror writer, as opposed to a legitimate literary figure. Even those who praise his work often do so under some kind of proviso, as though they are unexpectedly (or even accidentally) good, or in Trent's words, better written than you might imagine.

This dismissal of the genre can be seen throughout both literary and cinematic institutions. Horror novels and films may regularly top the best-seller list or make a killing at the box office, but rarely do they scoop awards or make it into critical lists. Similarly, horror movies (along with comedies) are frequently snubbed come awards season, and when one does slip through it is seen as an anomaly. Then there are those filmmakers who claim their most infamous genre works are not horror films at all, as though to be tarred with that brush would devalue their achievements in some way. Discussing *The Exorcist*, William Friedkin explained, '*When I set out to make this film I knew it wasn't a horror film… I know that it's on all these lists of horror films and I accept that, but only because I know that it just shows people's need to categorise it*' (Friedkin in Kermode, 1998), a sentiment which has also been echoed by the film's star, Linda Blair. Even William Peter Blatty has shied away from the term horror, instead describing the film as a 'supernatural detective story'. It seems that even those behind one of the most iconic horror films of all time are quick to deny its genre roots, doing anything they can to avoid the dreaded 'h' word. Perhaps such (possibly phony) evasion is one of the reasons that the film is held in such high regard by the mainstream?

Further to this, not only are horror films deemed culturally reductive among certain circles, there is also the fear that they can have a damaging effect on their viewers, resulting in copycat killings or similar acts of violence. A notorious example came when the pre-teen killers of British toddler James Bulger in 1993 were alleged to have been influenced by *Child's Play 3* (1991). While such accusations were quickly dismissed as hysterical scaremongering (a hysteria not dissimilar to paranoia around audience susceptibility and madness supposedly provoked by gothic novels), the British tabloids were quick to jump on the case, the right-wing likes of the Daily Mail printing reactionary headlines urging readers to '*Burn your video nasties*', calling for a ban on all horror films which could corrupt impressionable young minds. In Carpenter's film, Cane's horror fiction is claimed to affect his more unstable readers, resulting in '*disorientation, memory loss and severe paranoid reaction*'. Or, in the case of Cane's agent, psychotic outbreaks. Carpenter is not just responding to the ongoing cultural disregard for horror, but responding to preposterous accusations that it can be sociologically damaging. He does so by taking its supposed threats to the most extreme degree possible, creating a scenario in which a piece of pulp horror fiction is so potent it can drive everyone to insanity and ultimately end the world. Such a far-fetched proposition, in effect, renders such lazy, reactive, and sensational fears about horror obsolete. Carpenter is a frustrated filmmaker giving the finger to a conservative – and idiotic – establishment.

While *In the Mouth of Madness* asks that the horror genre be taken seriously, Trent's claim that Cane is merely a cash cow for his publishing house is not entirely without basis. Inside of Arcane Publishing we see countless pieces of Cane memorabilia – posters, T-shirts, mugs, etc. Cane can be purchased in more than just print form, and it is evident that he is a multi-million dollar business and his fans must be exploited in whatever way possible. For his publisher, Cane is everything. Even the name of the publishing house, in addition to sounding like Lovecraft's Arkham, also sounds like 'our Cane', as though the company own not just the rights to his work, but to his entire being. He is their property, in both mind and body. It is worth noting that *In the Mouth of Madness* was distributed by New Line, the studio behind the *A Nightmare on Elm Street* franchise. So successful were the *Elm Street* films, the once failing New Line studio was jokingly referred to as 'The House that Freddy built'. Arcane is in all senses the house that Cane built, and the Cane memorabilia strewn about the place recalls the sheer volume of Freddy tie-ins that came out during the 1980s, ranging from clothes to toys and video games, spin-off TV shows and even an automated Freddy hotline.

A piece of Sutter Cane memorabilia

In the Mouth of Madness hits its peak of self-reflexivity at the climax when Trent, upon leaving the asylum to find a world in ruins, stumbles into a cinema screening the movie adaptation of Cane's latest book. Outside of the cinema we see a poster for the film, which includes a credit block exactly as it would appear on the real poster of Carpenter's film, but with one significant difference, the actors' names are replaced with those of the characters they play. As Trent sits back and watches the movie, he sees his own image on the screen as the events of his recent life are played back to him. If we are in any doubt that what we have been watching is a fictional construct, now we can be absolutely sure. We witness Trent tip over into insanity as he watches his own descent into madness on the screen in front of him. If Cane's fiction is a deadly contagion, then the most effective medium by which to transmit it is not the written word at all, but through film. The final moments demonstrate that the extensive popularity of cinema offers the ultimate weapon of choice for any intergalactic demon wanting to bring about a human apocalypse. 'What about people who don't read', Dr Wrenn asks Trent, who has explained the danger of the book. 'There's a movie', Trent replies, with a knowing smile.

That Trent's insanity is portrayed through laughter is of significance too. Laughter can often be a product of discomfort. A horror film will frequently elicit spontaneous

A cinema showing the movie version of Cane's book

nervous giggles from its audience; the gasp of a jump scare immediately followed
by chuckles in recognition of the manipulation which has just occurred. While such
reactions might demonstrate the effectiveness of a film, there is nothing more damning
for a straight horror film than for it to be laughed at. Seen this way, laughter could
represent the ultimate insult to horror, a damning expression of its impotence and
another example of how the genre is not taken seriously. While Trent begins his journey
dismissive of horror, derisively unconvinced of its worth, by the end he is all too aware
of the power it holds. His laughter in the final frames is no longer mocking, but an all-
consuming, involuntary reaction, borne not simply from fear, but also the realisation that
he has no control and that everything up until now has meant nothing. His is a nihilistic
(or should that be cosmicistic?) laughter, that can only come once he has truly grasped
the far-reaching (intergalactic) horrors of the situation.

Trent's climactic trip to the movies stands as one of cinema's bleakest examples of
mise-en-abyme. The basic device is a familiar one, seen in works as diverse as *Singin' in
the Rain* (1952), which houses the fictional musical 'The Dancing Cavalier', or *The Last
Action Hero* (1993) which features within it the action packed 'Jack Slater IV'. Like *In the
Mouth of Madness*, the make-believe movie at the heart of Woody Allen's *The Purple
Rose Of Cairo* (1985) shares its name with the film itself, although unlike Carpenter's film,
the edges between the two works are quite clearly defined by Allen's decision to shoot
one of them in black and white. Notable examples of horror films which employ the
same gimmick include or *Demons* (1985) and *Popcorn* (1991), both of which take place

in cinemas where the celluloid horrors leap off the screen and into the auditoria. Bigas Luna's *Anguish* (1987) takes this concept even further. In Luna's film, we begin with the understanding we are watching a straightforward horror narrative about a homicidal killer, only to realise the movie in question is actually playing at a cinema for the enjoyment of an entirely new group of characters who occupy an alternate cinematic universe. But sure enough the two worlds collide as the events on screen begin to bleed into the 'real' world of the movie theatre. At the mind-bending climax it is revealed that this film within a film is actually within *another* film, and as the credits roll we witness the audience of this third picture leave their seats and exit the theatre. The notion that the cinema screen (or the flimsy page of a book) is unable to contain the potency of the stories projected onto it is expanded upon in Carpenter's film in a 'blink and you'll miss it' moment during one of the rapid fire montage sequences, in which we see the woman from the painting that hangs in the lobby of the Pickman Hotel literally emerging from the frame. Like the creatures in *Demons*, for example, or the monsters in Cane's work, she has been liberated from her artistic prison and into the real world. Like both cinema and literature, painting too has the power to break free and fully envelop its audience.

Ultimately Carpenter's film has so many layers of reality (or fiction) it almost risks imploding on itself with sheer self-reflexivity, collapsing under the weight of its cleverness. Here we have a book within a book within a film within a film, ultimately leaving the viewer unsure as the whether the film's main protagonist ever existed in the first place (existed within the film, at least; of course, he never really exists – he's a movie character after all). The layering of (un)reality can be clearly witnessed during Trent's dream early on in the film. He imagines returning to an alleyway he had previously visited in his waking life, where he saw two cops beating a man to the ground. In his dream reinterpretation he concocts an even more disturbing version of events, in which hordes of disfigured onlookers gather and one of the cops is revealed to have a hideously deformed face. Trent suddenly wakes up. It was all a dream. But then in a jump scare ripped straight out the climax of his own *Prince of Darkness*, Carpenter reveals the monster cop is sitting next to him on the sofa. Suddenly he wakes again. It was all a dream, within a dream. Here we are presented with four versions of reality – the first occurrence, the dream interpretation, the dream within the dream, and finally Trent's waking reality. Under the influence of Cane, imagination and unreality rule, so how can

Trent's dream within a dream

we ever be really sure of what we are seeing? Once again, we think of the opening sequence in which Trent, who is for all intents and purposes insane, recounts the horrors of his experience in Hobb's End. How can we know that the tale which follows is anything other than a madman's fantasy? Similarly, when Trent and Styles arrive in Hobb's End, Trent is actually asleep. As they pass through the mysterious tunnel, and out into the sun-drenched idyll of Cane's hometown, could we not simply be in Trent's unconscious mind? Interestingly, the tunnel from which Trent and Styles emerge on 'the other side', recalls the bridge through which the Maitlands plummet to their deaths in Tim Burton's *Beetlejuice* (1988). Like the tunnel in Carpenter's film, Burton's also serves as an entry point to another world. For the protagonists in *Beetlejuice* that other world is the afterlife, but for Trent and Styles it is an alternate dimension. Or perhaps, in Trent's case, it is merely a dream. Could the events which follow simply be the nightmare of a man who has just binged on too many scary books? Fantasy and reality, madness and sanity, waking life and dreams – everything is interchangeable. Once again, all bets are off.

But for all its thematic intricacies and narrative trickery, the fine line between reality and unreality is perhaps most compellingly captured in a fleeting moment towards the end of the film, just before Trent kills the man at the book shop. He peers into the shop window, his own image reflected in the glass. Inside the window is a cardboard cut-out of Trent, used to promote Cane's novel, while copies of the novel itself are visible on the shelves inside the store. Carpenter presents us with a multitude of Trents, but the question of which, if any, is the real one, is up for debate. The Trent outside the shop represents the man we have followed throughout the film. The one reflected in the window is the fictional Trent, his likeness rendered on a flat screen as it is at the film's movie theatre climax. The cardboard cut-out is Cane's creation, the version of Trent that exists within the writer's head, while the small Trent visible on the book covers is the version of him that exists within the printed page. Here we witness Trent both as real and as imagined, a fragmented man split into different parts. He is everywhere yet he is nowhere, a figment of another man's imagination who cannot exist in his own right. For a film that dabbles in such existential complexities, it is a testament to both De Luca's writing and Carpenter's direction that the film is so comprehensible. As opposed to the deliberately perplexing world of, say, Christopher Nolan's *Inception* (2010), in which multiple layers of reality also exist, *In the Mouth of Madness* tries its best to be clear in its presentation of a variety of truths and universes. In a film which is ultimately about the loss of control for all those who exist within it, Carpenter maintains a steadfast grip on the material, presiding over events with authoritative command.

The many faces of Trent

CHAPTER 7: 'THIS ONE WILL DRIVE YOU ABSOLUTELY MAD'

Trent: Believe me, the sooner we're off the planet, the better.

Styles: Now you sound like Cane.

Trent: No, not me. You're the Cane lover.

Styles: I just like being scared. Cane's work scares me.

Trent: What's to be scared about? It's not like it's real or anything.

Styles: It's not real from your point of view, and right now reality shares your point of view. What scares me about Cane's work is what might happen if reality shared his point of view.

Trent: Whoa. We're not talking about reality here. We're talking about fiction. It's different, you know.

Styles: A reality is just what we tell each other it is. Sane and insane could easily switch places. If the insane were to become the majority you would find yourself locked in a padded cell wondering what happened to the world.

Trent: No, that wouldn't happen to me.

Styles: It would if you realised everything you ever knew was gone. It'd be pretty lonely being the last one left.

A number of philosophical threads have run throughout this book so far, from epistemological and ontological concerns about the stability (or instability) of a universal truth, and the nihilistic idea that all knowledge is contingent (and nothing really means anything) which exists at the heart of postmodernism. But while we have touched upon these weighty concepts, the above exchange between Trent and Styles on their drive to Hobb's End perhaps represents the philosophical heart of Carpenter's film, and thus serves as a fitting starting point for a more focused examination on the philosophy of *In the Mouth of Madness*.

Parallels between the existential preoccupations of *In the Mouth of Madness* and *The Matrix* have already been drawn, and in many ways this dialogue once again recalls a scene in the latter in which Morpheus questions the flimsy concept of reality. '*Have you ever had a dream, Neo, that you were so sure was real? What if you were unable to wake from that dream? How would you know the difference between the dream world and the real world?'* In both of these exchanges, reality is not an absolute that can be reliably perceived, it is something we agree upon collectively. It takes a mad person – or a prophet – to see through the flimsiness of 'consensus reality'. Both *The Matrix* and *In the Mouth of Madness* work with the exciting dramatic potential of this idea, adding in a dash of malevolence to Cartesian scepticism – what if some external, evil force were constructing the veil of reality upon which duped masses the agreed upon? Crucially, though, Carpenter does not create a crusading action film that re-installs a sense of stable, authentic reality once this veil has been lifted, as the Wachowskis did. Instead, he crafts a more obtuse, surreal cinematic vision of what we might call Cartesian paranoia – crucially, a *horror* film. Theorist Eugene Thacker argues for horror's unique ability to look directly at the face of otherwise incomprehensible desolation of ontological stability: *'Horror is about the paradoxical thought of the unthinkable'* (Thacker, 2011: 2). Whilst the power of horror as social and political commentary has previously been discussed, Thacker's proposal goes further: for him, horror is a mode of philosophical enquiry. That is not to say that it *'contain[s] the type of logical rigor that one finds in the philosophy of Aristotle or Kant'* but it is *'a non-philosophical attempt to think about the world-without-us philosophically'* (2011: 9). *In the Mouth of Madness* is not a philosophical treatise and neither Carpenter or De Luca (nor myself for that matter!) are philosophers. But with its focus on shaky realities, unfathomable other dimensions – and the human terror when faced with these – we can say that *In the Mouth of Madness* exemplifies the way Thacker accounts for the capacities of horror.

Trent and Styles' conversation about the nature of reality neatly sums up the film's ontological provocations: the idea that – with a shift in perception – the sane could become the insane, reality could become fiction, existence could become non-existence. Carpenter registers such provocations in the narrative structures, style and mood of the film, resulting in a dreamlike (or nightmarish) quality more akin to the surrealist works of David Lynch or the abstract logic of Adrian Lyne's *Jacob's Ladder* (1990), than we might traditionally expect from Carpenter. The observation from the man in the Hobb's End tavern, that *'reality is not what it used to be'*, slyly encapsulates this shift in Carpenter's approach, and the resulting narrative and stylistic techniques (non-linear storytelling, shifting viewpoints, quick-fire montage) he employs to disorientate and unnerve the viewer. In a departure from the more conventional Carpenter narrative structure that fans might be accustomed to, here he experiments more freely with deviating timeframes and unreliable perspectives. This is undeniably Carpenter's film, but his mode of expression seems different, twisted, making for a discomforting experience. As the film progresses, our faith in the characters and our ability to trust their actions is slowly stripped away. By the end of the film we are not sure if we can even trust Carpenter himself. He has not merely blurred the line between fantasy and reality, as much as he has destroyed it completely. Conventional logic (by Carpenter's standards) is no longer valid, we have entered another realm, a Lovecraftian dimension beyond the reach of human perception. Essentially the film is one big game, and we, the audience, have been duped.

Styles' comments regarding subjective perspectives also throws up the question of whose point of view the film is taken from. We are initially led to believe this is Trent's tale, that what we are watching is the story he is recounting to his doctor at the asylum. How is it, then, that we often leave Trent, witnessing events at which he was not present? How could he possibly know what happened when Styles went to the Black Church since he was not there to witness it? Could this really be the subjective narrative of a madman, who is filling in the gaps, or perhaps even just fabricating events? Or are such gaps in narrative logic confirmation that this is Cane's point of view, and that Trent is simply a fictional character in his book? If viewed as merely a work of fiction it should not matter if the components do not quite add up. What's a plot hole or two when we're talking about the end of the world?

This is a film designed to disorientate throughout, and one of the ways it achieves this is in the persistent manipulation of time, which Carpenter bends and ultimately renders obsolete. Carpenter's uncharacteristically non-linear approach is evident from the outset. The opening scenes of the film are part of a framing device. We are not starting at the beginning, but at the end; the majority of the film to be presented in the form of a lengthy flashback. This makes the use of the Carpenters' song even more amusing, with their sentiment that 'We've only just begun' ringing completely false. We have not just begun, nowhere near; in fact, we are at the end. Not just at the end of the film from a linear perspective, but essentially at the end of humanity. With this in mind the seemingly innocuous lyrics take on a deeply chilling, ironic poignancy.

Styles' comments on the car journey also highlight the distorted structure of the film. She says that if unreality took over, Trent would find himself *'locked in a padded cell wondering what happened to the world'*. Of course, this is exactly what ends up happening. But since we have already seen this, Style's prediction actually becomes a reference to what has come before. This might seem like a maddening plot spoiler – not only do we know that Trent ends up mad and alone in an apocalyptic world, but that the 'insane' do in fact take over. However, in this moment it becomes clear the conclusion does not matter as much as the manner in which we arrive there. There can be no surprise ending in a film that is essentially one protracted twist.

It is during this drive that Trent and Styles first encounter the recurring figure of an old man on a bike. The man, who cycles past them several times in a manner which defies understood logic of space and time, appears unnaturally aged, a grotesque vision of decrepitude. It soon becomes clear that this is no ordinary old man when, having been hit by the car, he begins to speak with the voice of a much younger person. This disconnect between what we see and what we hear is a common thematic device employed throughout the film, adding to a sense that time is distorted and breaking apart. It also draws our attention to the technical trickery (or magic) of cinema. Image and sound are not fused as in reality, they are separate, separable and manipulable. Once again, the unreality of film is placed at the forefront (the narrative of *In the Mouth of Madness* features layers of unreality, and the film itself is one of these). The old man's body has aged (almost perversely so) but his voice has remained youthful. It is one of the film's most unsettling moments (possibly even more so than the vivid scenes of horror that will follow), highlighting the cruelty of time, and the devastating way it ravages the corporeal body. The young voice says *'I can't get out'*, and while it is likely he is referring to Hobb's End, or the repetitive cycle he is forced to repeat, it could also be that he cannot escape his body, which has become a prison to him. In a film which broadly deals with 'the end', it reminds us that life is finite, and eventually we will all reach our own personal apocalypse. Given the description of the man ravaged by age, it may seem an unfortunate time to point out that this elderly figure bears more than a passing resemblance to John Carpenter himself, with his long grey hair, receding hairline and faded denim attire. That Carpenter should resemble this harbinger of passing time is a nice touch. As an artist working in a time-based medium, Carpenter is messing with

Old father time

chronology and enjoying it, manipulating the order and shape of time, unsettling and confusing the audience. Here he essentially casts himself as 'old father time', the physical embodiment of the temporal, frequently represented throughout art and literature as an elderly male. The implication is even more apparent when we notice the playing card in the spokes of the old man's bicycle: a joker. As is the case throughout the film, Carpenter is playing with us, although at least here he has the decency to let us in on the gag.

Elsewhere, the distinction between young and old is blurred time and time again. The first time we see Cane, he appears from behind the doors of the Black Church. Initially we see a young boy standing in the entrance, only for the doors to close and rapidly reopen to reveal the adult Cane is his place. In another scene, the gang of strange children who roam about Hobb's End are seen to be disfigured and deformed. One of them, a young girl of around 10 years old, in addition to the multiple lacerations on her face, appears to be horribly aged, her youthful glow no longer apparent. Once again, these moments not only show a disorientating breakdown of time in which someone can age decades in the blink of an eye, but also the effects of time of the human body. Time should be feared, and in Cane's (and Carpenter's) world, it must not be trusted.

While rapid onset of time is seen frequently during the film, the reverse is also evident in Carpenter's uncharacteristic use of slow motion, a technique he employs during several sequences which take place in Hobb's End – our first encounter with the group of children, or the dog attack at the Black Church, for example. *In the Mouth of Madness* was actually the first time Carpenter used slow motion (an obvious way in which a director can control and manipulate time), having previously expressed a disdain for the technique as being 'dishonest'. It makes perfect sense that he should use it here, in a film which is all about deception and subterfuge. Carpenter uses a very subtle slow motion, so as to make the sequences feel strangely off, rather than obviously slowed down, which again lends a mysterious quality to the town, as though it exists outside of the boundaries of conventional time.

If time is unstable in Carpenter's twisted cinematic dreamscape, it is not just in the order and speed in which images unfold onscreen. The images themselves are manipulated, and distorted; the reliability of visual perception is thrown into dispute. It seems that multiple registers of perception – the passage of time, the appearance of space and matter – upon which we rely to comprehend the universe outside our minds, are under attack. The film is called *In the Mouth of Madness*, but 'In the Eyes of Madness' might be the more accurate title, considering the extent to which insanity is implied in terms of faulty or altered visual perceptions. In the scene when Cane tears himself apart, Carpenter uses a ripple effect, manipulating the way we receive the images, unsettling our powers of visual comprehension. Traditionally such an effect is used to signify a dream sequence or fantasy scene. It is a slightly outdated gimmick, perhaps most readily associated with old movies or television soap operas. It seems to imply that there is an element of fantasy to the whole scene (once again, is Trent dreaming?), but also that this outer dimension exists on another plane, and we must adjust our vision to be able to see it. Like his use of slow motion, Carpenter is distorting the image, playing tricks with our eyes, and letting us know that we cannot trust what we see.

De Luca's dialogue is littered throughout with references to the act of looking or seeing. In an attempt to disprove Styles' theory that they are in Cane's fictional Hobb's End, a sceptical Trent points out of his hotel window, exclaiming, '*You see, reality*'. Although, of course, Styles soon proves his reality is false – sight can no longer be relied upon. When Cane is telling Trent about his latest work, he mentions that it '*helps you see*', drawing attention to the anxieties around unreliable visual perception. The mention of sight is not confined to the spoken dialogue either. When Trent is in the alleyway, under the early effects of Cane's influence, a piece of graffiti is visible on the wall, ominously proclaiming, '*I can see*'. It could be apt to describe Cane, as master of his universe, as omniscient as well as omnipotent. He sees all. Trent, on the other hand, sees little.

Ominous graffiti

Not simply functioning on a level of subjective perception (or suggestion), throughout the film we can literally see how the eyes of those who read Cane's work are physically affected (or infected) by his prose. We first notice this when the man we later learn to be Cane's agent attacks Trent with an axe. In a close up of his face, we see his irises appear split, the two halves connected but clearly distinct from each other, like optic Siamese twins. It is an unnerving effect, which shows the literal way in which Cane's work changes your perspective. In this case, the double iris represents a kind of second sight, as though there are two ways of looking (the one of our world, and the one of the vast dimensions beyond it) and by reading Cane's work you are given the gift of extra sensory (extra-dimensionary?) perception. However, such intergalactic clairvoyance is too much for the human brain to comprehend, and with it comes madness. Cane's work first opens your eyes, and then destroys your mind. Trent himself, who has thus far had no exposure to Cane's work, is immune to its power, unable to see the threat of the so-called horror crap he is so quick to dismiss. As the axe-wielding maniac approaches him, appearing to the viewer from behind a bus advertising Cane's upcoming 'In the Mouth of Madness', Trent is facing the opposite direction, unable to see him. It is a classic pantomime moment – 'he's behind you' the audience want to shout, much like during the climactic scare in *Halloween* when, unbeknownst to Laurie, the supposedly dead Michael Myers sits up in the background, as she sobs quietly in the foreground. For now, Trent is blissfully unaware of his impending doom, which will eventually shatter his world like an axe crashing through a glass window.

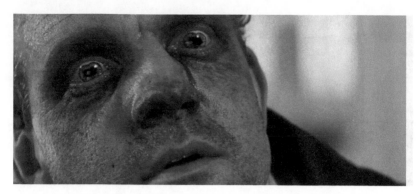

The disfigured eyes of Cane's former agent

We continue to see Cane's work corrupt the eyes of its readers throughout the film. When Trent goes to a bookshop to buy copies of Cane's books for research purposes, one of his fans utters '*He can see you*'. The reader in question, a pasty-faced, unwell-looking young man, wears glasses. While glasses are traditionally understood to correct an ocular deficiency, in this case it could be that he now sees the world through a Caneian filter. As is the case for Nada in *They Live*, whose access to special sunglasses reveals the terrifying truth of the world around him, the bespectacled boy can see clearly, unlike Trent who is yet to be shown the way.

When Cane's influence does impact on Trent, however, the effects are quite immediate. Returning home from his initial meeting at Arcane, Trent immerses himself in Cane's work, reading through the night, slowly beginning to understand the appeal (and power) of his prose. At one point, Trent puts down the book he is reading and, noticeably tired, rubs his eyes, the ink stains on his fingers leaving black marks around them. The text has already begun to change him, to transfer off the printed page and quite literally leave its mark on his body. With the black smudges around his eyes, Trent has been infected by Cane's work, which has polluted his vision and transformed his physical appearance. Suddenly in this moment Trent notices something – a design on the covers of Cane's books, which when cut out form a map of Hobb's End, thus providing the key to his whereabouts. It is only after Cane has gotten to Trent's eyes that Trent is able to see the clues. As with the rest of Cane's readers, his eyes have been opened and he is receptive to the truth. Of course, this is Cane's truth, not Trent's, and everything is part of a

Trent's ink-stained eyes

predestined set of events. At this point Trent believes he has control, that he is making connections on his own, but by now Cane's work is controlling his mind. Cane has not just expanded Trent's mind, but completely taken it over.

It seems that no one is safe from the transformative powers of Cane's work. Mrs Pickman, the seemingly sweet old lady who runs the inn at which Trent and Styles stay during their time in Hobb's End, first appears quite normal in appearance. However, just before Trent sees that she is one of 'them', a shapeshifting beast who has her husband handcuffed naked behind the reception desk, we see her eyes are red and tired, as though she has been rubbing them, like Trent did, after a long night spent reading. Later in the film, Cane shows the manuscript of his latest work to Styles, who as a result witnesses a succession of violent images of what has been and what is to come. She emerges from the experience with blood running from both of her eyes, as if physically assaulted by Cane's words, which have infected and mutated her. The image of bleeding eyes is repeated again near the end of the film, when the man who Trent kills at the bookshop also has blood leaking from his tear ducts.

The ways in which Cane's work can affect one's perception of the world is most visibly illustrated in the scene where Trent, having apparently escaped from Hobb's End, falls asleep on a coach taking him back to New York. He imagines Cane sitting next to him, informing Trent that his favourite colour is blue. Trent awakens to see the world around him as if through a blue lens. He screams and wakes up, his vision reverted to 'normal'.

The bleeding eyes of Cane readers

Through the mere power of suggestion Cane can shift how you see your surroundings. It initially appears that Carpenter shoots the scene though a blue filter, or adjusted the colours in post-production, but it is clear on closer inspection that the sets and actors were actually turned blue for the scene – the upholstery of the seats, the clothes and hair of the passengers, etc., are all varying shades of blue. It might seem a huge amount of work for such a brief scene, but the effect is very powerful and appropriately disorienting, further illustrating the extent to which Cane can alter the very fabric of one's subjective reality. Further to this, and in one of the film's more subliminal touches, at this point the more perceptive viewer might realise that everyone in the film is shown in close up to have blue eyes. Also, the film's closing credits are blue text on a black background, as opposed the more conventional white on black. Once again, Cane has not just infected the eyes of the entire population, turning them blue, but ultimately he has gotten to the viewers of Carpenter's film too. Perhaps the credits really are white on black, we just are no longer able to see them that way. After all, that is what the movie is there for, to get to those who have not yet read the book.

In *Hellraiser*, Pinhead informs one of the characters, and by extension the viewer, 'We have such sights to show you.' In the world of both that film and Carpenter's, the eyes have the power to gain us entry to another world, to look beyond the traditional limits of human perception and experience what exists beyond. Eyes, as the old cliché would have us believe, are the windows to the soul. However, in these films they are also the windows to another dimension, which, once seen, can never truly be escaped from. Like *In the Mouth of Madness*, *Hellraiser* does not reveal its most hideous, unfathomable (Lovecraftian?) monsters until the portal to another world has been opened. In the former this is when Kirsty plays with the puzzle box in her hospital room, in the latter when Cane tears himself open. The otherworldly beast is a common theme throughout Clive Barker's work (both cinematic and literary) as evidenced in the multitude of creatures that inhabit his film *Nightbreed*, about an underground community of exiled beasts. But while Barker's monsters are presented as real, those in *In the Mouth of Madness* could simply all be works of fiction – either the creations of a science fiction writer, or the vivid dreams of a man suffering from spooky story overexposure. Or perhaps even the hallucinations of a drugged up madman, locked up in an asylum, strung out on morphine? Like a hallucinogenic drug, Cane's work is said to 'open your mind'. Maybe we never really left Trent's cell room from the film's opening scenes. We are shown the sights, but it is not clear if our eyes can be trusted.

Another film that *In the Mouth of Madness* evokes in its depiction of what it means to lose sight of reality is David Cronenberg's *Videodrome* (1982), which depicts a mind-altering television channel, whose graphic images of torture and sadomasochism appear to have delusional effects on its viewers. Like Cane's work, Videodrome controls the minds of those exposed to it, forming a worldwide conspiracy to infect the entire population. Carpenter does for books what Cronenberg did for television, highlighting the arts as the most powerful weapon of communication that we have. Also rather Cronenbergian is the scene in which we enter Cane's inner sanctum within the Black Church. The moist, red walls themselves seem fleshy in appearance, organic and veiny, placing us within a muscular, physical entity, much like the set of Cronenberg's fictional

TV show. It is a scene of almost metaphysical body horror, as though the ephemeral concepts of thought and creativity have taken on a grotesque corporeal form. At this point we can be nowhere else but in Cane's mind, both metaphorically and literally. He even says to Styles, 'You can edit this one from the inside, looking out', as though we are not just in his head, but seeing through his eyes too. Styles is in Cane's mind, and as such he has taken full control of hers.

In addition to the increasing unreliability of visual perception, Carpenter also plays with visual and narrative repetition to generate a sense of growing unease and displacement for the viewer. Throughout the course of the film things or people appear, only to reappear again and again. Axes feature throughout the film. There is the axe used by Cane's agent and later the axe Mrs Pickman uses to kill her husband. We see a bloody axe abandoned on the streets of Hobb's End, while there is the axe that Trent himself uses to kill the man at the bookshop, almost bringing us full circle. Meanwhile, bicycles begin and end Trent's trip to Hobb's End. Before arriving in the town he sees the old man on the bike, while upon leaving he asks a paperboy for directions. The concept of repetition is unavoidable here, presented quite literally as a cycle. Elsewhere, the aforementioned crucifixes and strange children are just a couple of the other recurring motifs we see throughout. Much of the horror in The Apocalypse Trilogy is, of course, impending, inevitable annihilation. But in these cases horror emerges from non-teleological depictions of time. Repetitions keep us trapped in the same spot, creating the feeling that time is cyclical and cannot be outrun. When Trent attempts to leave Hobb's End, he drives in the same direction, yet somehow always ends up back in the centre of town. The same sequence is played to us three times in a row (by the third we the audience feel as though we are going mad too), and it seems Trent might be stuck in this perpetual pattern. Was this what the old man with the young voice was referring to when he said that he 'can't get out'? Like him, Trent could be trapped in this psychic loop forever, forced to repeat the same actions over and over again – his horrific end is not an end at all, it is perpetual, repetitive movement. Ultimately, the only way he can get out of it is to crash his car, which frees him temporarily from the circle like a sleeper experiencing a hypnic jerk, allowing him to progress onto somewhere else. This sequence is reminiscent of a dream scene in A Nightmare on Elm Street 4: Dream Master, when the heroine is locked in a cycle in which she keeps ending up in the same place, which might support the theory that what we are witnessing is all a product of Trent's unconscious. There is also a touch of the *The Twilight Zone* ('*a fifth dimension beyond that which is known to man*'), itself a rather Lovecraftian concept. As Trent finds himself trapped in his endless loop, he occupies his own personal twilight zone, the space between reality and unreality, a purgatory for the unconscious mind.

Trent finds himself in another hellish cycle later in the film. Upon returning to the 'real' world he ditches the manuscript he has been told by Cane to deliver to his publishers, only to have it inexplicably returned to him. He proceeds to burn the pages, hoping to ensure it will be destroyed forever, but when he returns to Arcane he is informed the manuscript was delivered months before and the novel has already been published. Despite his best efforts, Trent is unable to escape his own fate, forced in an endless chain of repetition until he understands he must simply do as he is instructed (like an actor performing the lines in their script). As we have been told repeatedly, in Cane's universe there is no free will. Trent is no more able to avoid his destiny than he is able to leave Hobb's End or rid himself of the cursed manuscript.

It is Trent's climactic trip to the cinema that provides the film's final cycle. As the movie plays on the screen we are right back at the beginning, with Trent in the asylum, screaming for his freedom. Now Trent, and the viewer too, is forced to relive the events all over again. And, of course, at the conclusion of the film Trent is watching in the cinema, the onscreen Trent will take a seat and watch himself play out the events that have just occurred, and so on, forever. It is a never ending cinematic Russian doll, a film within a film, within a film, within a film, within a film, and so on…

Given its propensity for repetition and nightmarish logic of its conclusion, it is quite fitting then that *In the Mouth of Madness* is a film that benefits from multiple viewings. So intricate are the complexities of its plot, and the richness of its concepts, that ultimately it is a work which demands more time and thought than any other film in Carpenter's canon. Perhaps that was his intention all along, to have us, like Trent, trapped in an endless cycle, watching the film over and over again, in a desperate attempt to unearth its secrets and explain its mysteries? Or perhaps we are never meant to understand it at all? Maybe, just maybe, it goes beyond the realm of pitiful human comprehension, and to fully embrace its full complexities would be the end of us all…

CONCLUSION: 'THIS IS A ROTTEN WAY TO END IT'

This book began with the suggestion that *In the Mouth of Madness* is a film in urgent need of critical re-evaluation. I proposed that John Carpenter's complex, tricksy creation was cruelly dismissed specifically because it *is* complex and it *is* tricksy. Hopefully, I have demonstrated how much it rewards those who take the time to wrestle with its complexities and decipher its tricks. But now that we have considered its rich webs of intertextuality, its postmodernist playfulness, its mediations on religious fanaticism, its existential philosophies, etc., we must ask: where do these disparate intellectual trajectories converge? What does it all add up to?

The preceding pages have built up to a claim that the horrors at the heart of *In the Mouth of Madness* stem from a kind of existential dread. The scares in this film do not manifest in the traditional forms of ghosts or masked maniacs, but in the notion that our otherwise solid understanding of reality and stable notions of existence – and, crucially the *meaning* of existing in this world, and our status as agents within it – are all just insubstantial collective delusions. But, as I wind up this book, I want to modify these weighty propositions somewhat. Yes, the film might be characteristic of a nineteenth-century Nietzschean nihilist – or, rather, a misanthropic Lovecraftian. But if *In the Mouth of Madness* were a person, it would not be a gloomy teen moping around with a copy of *Being and Nothingness* under their arm. No, Carpenter's film is just way too much fun for that. This is existential dread for the MTV generation – *In the Mouth of Madness* is a sardonic prankster, mischievous and energetic, out for trouble and a good time. Philosophically speaking, the film a frisky hybrid of nihilistic Lovecraftian cosmicism, and thoroughly playful 90s postmodernism – complete with joking genre references and deft sociological satire. The film may be dealing with some heavy philosophical shit, but it is important not to forget that part of the pleasure of Carpenter's horrific brand of postmodernism lies in its sense of independent, anarchic creativity. This may well be one of Carpenter's most fatalistic works, but at the same time it is one of his most perversely playful, and most joyous.

The narrative of *In the Mouth of Madness* positions artistic creativity as deadly, but the film as a whole can be read as a celebration of art and, more specifically, of horror as a devilish, yet legitimate, mode of intellectual expression. If Sutter Cane is the malevolent prophet, then John Carpenter (the real deity, pulling Cane's strings) is quite the opposite – he is here to entertain, to show his audience the time of their lives. As Trent bursts into laughter at the film's climax, we are allowed to join him, and to smile in recognition of the sheer inventiveness we have witnessed on screen. It's the end of the world as we know it, but we feel fine.

Perhaps, then, more than anything, *In the Mouth of Madness* is a film about storytelling. It is about the wonder, and mystery, and complexity of telling tales, and about the power that comes with it. These myths can thrill us as entertainment and enrich our lives intellectually. And they can also become 'scripture', and indoctrinate us. As such Cane, Lovecraft, King, Hubbard and therefore even Carpenter himself, are more than just yarn spinners – they are world builders, charismatic authorities attracting legions of followers, each united by the power they hold as creators of alternate realities. But whilst *In the Mouth of Madness* might initially place literature as the primary key to opening minds and unlocking the secrets of the universe, the climactic punchline in the movie theatre shows it is cinema which ultimately wields the greater power. And in making this significant shift, in the end it is the filmmaker, and not the writer, who is presented as the most powerful storyteller of all. And that is the gospel according to John Carpenter.

BIBLIOGRAPHY

Boulenger, Gilles (2003) *John Carpenter: The Prince of Darkness*. W. Hollywood, CA: Silman-James Press.

Canby, Vincent (1982) Review of *The Thing*, *The New York Times*, 25 June.

Carroll, Jonathan (n.d.) Interview. jonathancarroll.com.

Carroll, Noël (1990) *The Philosophy of Horror, or Paradoxes of the Heart*. London: Routledge.

Cherry, Brigid (2009) *Horror*. Abingdon: Routledge.

Colavito, Jason (2011) 'Cthulu vs Xenu: The Case of H.P. Lovecraft and Scientology's Cosmology', jasoncolavito.com.

Marie Mulvey-Roberts, Marie (2004) 'A Spook Ride on Film', in Ian Conrich and David Woods, *The Cinema of John Carpenter: The Technique of Terror*. London: Wallflower Press.

Cumbow, Robert C. (2000) *Order in the Universe: The Films of John Carpenter*. Lanham, Maryland: Scarecrow Press Inc.

Descartes, René (1637) *The Discourse on the Method*.

Ebert, Roger (1995) Review of *In the Mouth of Madness*, *Chicago Sun Times*, 3 February.

Elsworth, Catherine (2014) Interview with Stephen King, goodreads.com, November.

Grey, Orrin (2011) 'Cosmic Horror in John Carpenter's "Apocalypse Trilogy"', in *Strange Horizons*, 24 October.

Harrington, Richard (1987) Review of *Prince of Darkness*, *The Washington Post*, 28 October.

Kael, Pauline (1979) Review of *Halloween*, *The New Yorker*, 19 February 1979.

Kermode, Mark (1998) William Friedkin Interview, *The Guardian*.

King, Stephen (2000) *On Writing: A Memoir of the Craft*. London: Hodder and Stoughton.

Le Banc, Michelle and Odell, Colin (2011) *John Carpenter (Pocket Essentials)*. Harpenden: Kamera Books.

Lovecraft, H.P. (1936) 'At the Mountains of Madness', originally published in *Astounding Stories*, February-April.

Lovecraft, H.P. (1927) 'The Colour Out of Space', originally published in *Amazing Stories*, September.

Lovecraft, H.P. (1936) 'The Haunter of the Dark', originally published in *Weird Tales*, December.

Lovecraft, H.P. (1933) Letter to Richard Morse.

Lovecraft, H.P. (1927) Letter to Farnsworth Wright, 5 July.

Lovecraft, H.P. (1924) *The Rats in the Walls*, originally published in Weird Tales, March.

Lovecraft, H.P. (1927) *Supernatural Horror in Literature*.

Migliore, Andrew and Strysik, John (2006) *Lurker in the Lobby: A Guide to the Cinema of H.P. Lovecraft*. San Francisco: Night Shade Books.

Conrich, Ian and Woods, David (2004) *The Cinema of John Carpenter: The Technique of Terror*. London: Wallflower Press.

Phillips, Kendall R. (2012) *Dark Directions: Romero, Craven, Carpenter, and the Modern Horror Film*. Carbondale, Illinois: Southern Illinois University Press.

Roland, Paul (2014) *The Curious Case of H.P. Lovecraft*. London: Plexus.

Rowe, Michael (1994) 'What Terror Lies *In the Mouth of Madness*', *Fangoria*, #136, September.

Rowe, Michael (1995) 'Master of Madness', *Fangoria*, #140, March.

Salisbury, Mark (1995) Review: *In the Mouth of Madness*, *Fangoria*, #140, March.

Seibold, Witney (2013) Exclusive Interview: John Carpenter, craveonline.co.uk, 23 October.

Shelley, Mary (2003 [1831]) *Frankenstein, or the Modern Prometheus*. London: Penguin.

Thacker, Eugene (2011) *In the Dust of This Planet: Volume 1 of Horror of Philosophy*. London: Zero Books.

DEVIL'S ADVOCATES

"Auteur Publishing's new Devil's Advocates critiques on individual titles offer bracingly fresh perspectives from passionate writers. The series will perfectly complement the BFI archive volumes." Christopher Fowler, *Independent on Sunday*

HALLOWEEN

"Murray Leeder's thoughtful, clearly expressed analysis is far reaching in scope while resisting the temptation to become sidetracked... a joy to read; it's insightful and well researched and serves as an encouragement to return to *Halloween* once again" – *Exquisite Terror*

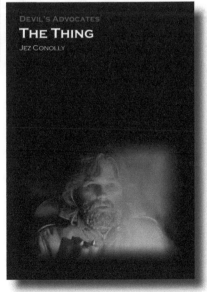

THE THING

"The hallmark for me of this sort of book is whether it makes me want to go back to the item under discussion to view it through new eyes, and there is certainly a lot in this, particularly about the choices that Carpenter makes in his framing of shots and the narrative, which does exactly that... A fascinating discussion about an often-maligned movie" – *Sci-Fi Bulletin*

BV - #0011 - 150819 - C0 - 190/140/6 - PB - 9781911325406